break
100
now!

break 100 now!

FROM HACKER TO GOLFER IN JUST 90 DAYS

**MIKE ADAMS AND T.J. TOMASI, PH.D.,
with MIKE CORCORAN**

A Mountain Lion Book

HarperPerennial
A Division of HarperCollinsPublishers

HarperCollins books may be purchased for educational, business, or sales promotional use. For information, please write to: Special Markets Department, HarperCollins Publishers, Inc., 10 East 53rd Street, New York, New York 10022.

FIRST EDITION

Library of Congress Cataloging-in-Publication Data
Adams, Mike, 1954–
    Break 100 now! : from hacker to golfer in just 90 days / Mike Adams and T.J. Tomasi with Mike Corcoran. — 1st ed.
       p. cm.
    "A Mountain Lion book."
    ISBN 0–06–273480–6
    1. Golf—Handbooks, manuals, etc. I. Tomasi, T.J. II. Corcoran, Mike. III. Title.
    GV965.A32 1998   97–26636
    796.352'3—dc21   CIP

00 01 02 ❖/RRD 10 9 8 7 6

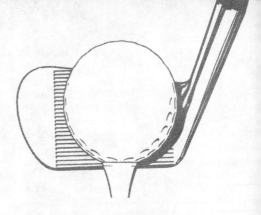

Contents

Introduction   vii

1 Here's the Plan   1

2 It's in the Bag (Or Sometimes It's the Arrow,
   Not the Archer)   5

3 The Short Road to Success   21

4 Course Management for Dummies
   (And a Few Tips on the Subject for
   Smart People Like You)   71

5 The Full Shots: Getting Ready Is the
   Most Important Part   97

6 Swinging for Power: You Swing
   the Club and the Club (Not You!) Hits the Ball   121

7 Practice: Forget the Excuses, We've Heard
   'Em All. If You Don't Practice, You Won't Improve.
   Here's How to Do It Without Wasting Your Time.   141

8 It's Time to Stop Reading and Start Doing   155

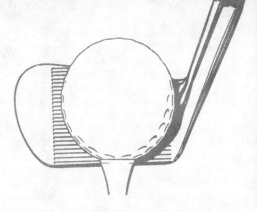

Introduction

This book is intended to improve your overall golf game, but it is written for a specific golfer—the one struggling to break 100. As such, it is organized in a rather unconventional manner.

Most golf instruction books start out with the fundamentals. This one doesn't, and the reason is simple: We assume you already play the game, and it would be ridiculous—and unrealistic—for us to expect you to stop playing and completely overhaul your game.

Starting with the fundamentals is the easiest way to organize a book, but since you already play, we've presented the information in the book in a manner that will allow you to see the quickest results to the bottom line (your score) with the lowest risk. There's very little chance that your game will actually be worse after you read this book. We hope you enjoy it.

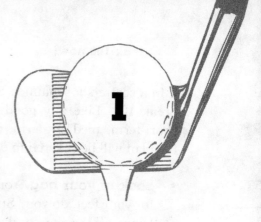

1

Here's the Plan

If you're reading this book for its intended purpose, you're not getting the most of what the game of golf has to offer. You might find it comforting to know that this fact numbers you among the vast majority. No accurate measure can be taken, but based on the information we put together on people who come to our golf schools and based on the best estimate of a number of leading teachers around the world, it appears likely that a full 80 percent of the people who play golf fail to break 100 on a regular basis. You can do better.

Improving your game—in this case, succeeding in regularly breaking 100—requires a commitment on your part. The commitment is not so vast that the decision to pursue the goal should involve a lot of deep soul searching, because it's easier to improve your game than you probably realize. In just about anything you do in life the chances of success increase if you create a well-thought-out plan and follow it. There's nothing profound about this thought—it's just plain common sense. If you want to improve your golf game, you won't succeed if you attempt to do it in a scattershot manner. So, friend, here's your 90-day plan to break 100. Like any good plan it builds upon itself and has short-term, medium-term, and long-term goals. Each point of the plan will be covered in detail in the subsequent chapters.

- **Look in your bag.** You don't wear shoes that are too small for your feet, do you? Suppose you have a size 34 waist (been laying off the cheesecake, heh?). Would it ever occur to you to try to wear a pair of size 28 trousers, or size 48 trousers? Of course not. The point is, it's rather silly to attempt to play golf if the clubs you use don't fit your body, game, or skill level. The typical golfer buys a set of clubs that the latest tour phenomenon is playing and then tries to adjust his swing to them. The fact is the club should fit your swing. The set makeup should also consist of clubs that will allow you to overcome shortcomings and take advantage of your talents. There's a good chance you can knock a bunch of strokes off your game simply by making certain you have clubs that fit you. And it's the easiest way to get started.

- **Hit the ball closer to the hole when you have a realistic chance to do so—which is quite often.** If you're a typical golfer (and we can assume you're not a PGA Tour player if you're reading this book), you play approximately 70 percent of your shots in a given round from 100 yards or closer to the hole. Generally speaking, the shorter the shot, the less complicated it is and the less room there is for error. Your chances of success increase on short shots, and you're playing a relatively short shot about 70 percent of the time. You can see that it makes sense to become more proficient from close range. This book will help you do that.

- **Be a better manager.** While nearly every golfer tends to ignore it, playing a round of golf is similar to any other pursuit that involves plotting a course of some sort. From this tactical perspective it's not all that different than sailing or playing chess—you have to see some sort of plan evolving in your head. Here's the good news: Plotting your way through each hole on a golf course is fairly simple—much easier than the aforementioned chess strategy, which requires you to take into consideration the brain and tendencies of your opponent. In golf, the course doesn't move or think. The only real variable with a somewhat consistent presence is wind. Modern maintenance techniques have allowed for almost every course to be in fine shape, eliminating what used to be another consistent variable. Course conditioning can now be lumped in with rain as an infrequent element of your tactical planning.

The biggest factor in setting your course is your own capabilities and knowledge of your limitations. Once you can get a handle on those you'll be plotting more successful campaigns than General Patton, and this book is just the battle plan you need.

• **Hit the ball farther (and straighter while you're at it).** Chances are you already wish to hit the ball a lot farther than you do—as do most golfers. Not everyone realizes the full extent to which added distance can help your game, however. Some people just want to hit it farther for the feeling of power. Others, because it makes other golfers say clever things like "Whooeee, you hit the snot out of that one." Even though you may have a vague idea that hitting a longer ball would improve your game, do you know by how much? In our schools at the Academy of Golf at PGA National, we demonstrate this to our students by playing a round with them wherein they begin play on each hole from the point to which the teacher has driven the ball. Counting the drive as their first shot, the student then finishes up the hole. Their scores for the round range (on average) between 10–20 shots better than they typically score.

Of course if you play Magellan golf—you're all over the map—it doesn't really matter how far you hit the ball, because it's tough to make good scores from the bottom of a lake or from behind the hot dog stand. So we'll fix you up with some ideas and strategies that will help you keep the ball in play.

- **Practice with a purpose.** Never in the history of sport has any game matched golf for the amount of ineffective and downright negative habits created during what the average golfer perceives to be practice. When most golfers think "practice," what they mean is pounding balls on the practice tee until their arms fall off, accomplishing little more than a rather subdued aerobic workout.

  Another tendency golfers have is to practice elements of their game at which they already excel. After all, who wants to watch one lousy shot after another fly off the clubface? So while there is a reason for this behavior (gratification), the reason makes about as much sense as Michael Jordan practicing his dribbling. It's safe to say he's got that down pat. Sure, some practice is needed on these things to keep your game at the level it's at, but your primary focus should be on improving the areas in which you are weak. This book will help you do that.

- **Work the plan.** Once you understand the plan, you'll need to implement it in a week-to-week manner, so you stay on track. The last part of this book will give you the plan in a calendar format.

- **Enjoy the game more than you do now.** This isn't part of the plan, it's just what will happen as a result of following it.

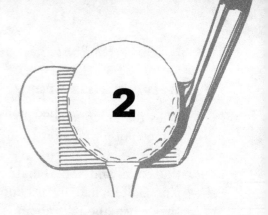

2

It's in the Bag

(OR SOMETIMES IT'S THE ARROW, NOT THE ARCHER)

In the game of golf, the clubs with which you strike the ball are your primary weapons. As such, they must be comfortable for you to handle and allow you to perform the task at hand without creating additional problems for you. Your set must also consist of clubs that allow you to maximize your strengths and bolster the weak areas of your game. Of all the goals in your overall plan to break 100 none is easier than making sure your clubs fit you and that your set is composed of the best selection of clubs for you. Having a set that fits you and your game requires two things: a look in your current bag combined with an honest assessment of your game, and just a few minutes (really) with a knowledgeable clubfitter.

Let's start with the driver, since that's the club you're currently most likely to reach for on the majority of the holes you play.

Driving Miss Crazy

With the emergence of the metal wood in the mid–1980s there came another phenomenon on the equipment scene: Some companies began stamping the degree of clubface loft on the sole of the club, and the remaining manufacturers quickly followed suit. Golfers had always known their clubs had loft on them, but they never thought about it in actual numbers. And, of course, applying actual numbers to the loft led the average golfer down the mistaken path that, unless he was a complete wimp, he should be playing the club with the least amount of loft, so his powerful drives would achieve maximum distance. It's sort of like the "stiff shaft syndrome" that causes otherwise sane people to believe they should play the strongest possible shaft lest their buddies will think of them as someone possessing less than the strength of 10 men.

At the root of "loftlexia" and "stiff shaft syndrome" is the absurd connection the average golfer makes between his own equipment and that of the highly skilled professional tour golfer, a connection made all the more believable in the minds of the average golfer by intense and expensive marketing campaigns on the part of club manufacturers. So when the average golfer started hearing about the pros hitting drivers with 9 degrees or 10 degrees of loft, he figured that's what was best for him. And he, Mr. Average Golfer, was dead wrong. The fact is, you may not need a driver at all, and you certainly don't need one with as little loft as a pro tour player uses. Nevertheless, the single biggest equipment mistake we see in the people who come to our schools is not enough loft on their driver.

Driver Considerations

So why is the amount of loft on your driver such a big deal? For starters, the less loft a club has, the more difficult it is to hit straight, because the lack of loft is more apt to create sidespin on the ball (causing a hook or slice) than it is to create backspin (which essentially allows the ball to fly straight). In addition, the lack of loft makes it more difficult to get the ball in the air for any sustained amount of time. And what are the two biggest ballstriking concerns for a golfer who can't break 100? Keeping the ball in the air for as long as possible (distance) and accuracy.

For this reason, the recommendation here is to use a driver with no less than 10.5 degrees of loft. However, the advantages of hitting a driver may not be readily applicable to you at this stage of your game development. There's a strong case to be made that you completely forget about the driver until your game is at a level that you can fully realize the potential of hitting one.

The alternative to the driver is to opt for the 3-wood as your main driving club. In terms of distance, there isn't that big of a difference between the two clubs, and the more lofted 3-wood is easier to control.

In terms of pure distance, a ball struck with a driver and a ball struck with a 3-wood will fly about the same distance in the air. The fact that the ball struck with the driver tends to run farther on the ground (due to its lower trajectory) isn't necessarily such a huge advantage that you should automatically eliminate the 3-wood as your driving weapon of choice. Consider:

- The difference in actual distance between a typical driver and typical 3-wood is only about 8 yards with a clubhead speed of up to 85 mph. Beyond 85 mph, the difference goes up to about 12 total yards. The average 3-wood has four degrees more loft than the average driver and is a half-inch shorter, so the difference in distance performance is something akin to comparing your 5-iron to your 6-iron. However, the 3-wood is a higher, more controlled shot that has a higher likelihood of finding its target. The average golfer is 56 percent more accurate with a 3-wood than he is with a driver.

- Most fairways are between 35–50 yards wide, which leaves a lot of room for error once you learn how to aim (which is covered later on). Testing has proved that a 3-wood will curve off line a maximum of 30 yards if the club is moving at 130 mph at impact. Chances are, your club isn't going to be

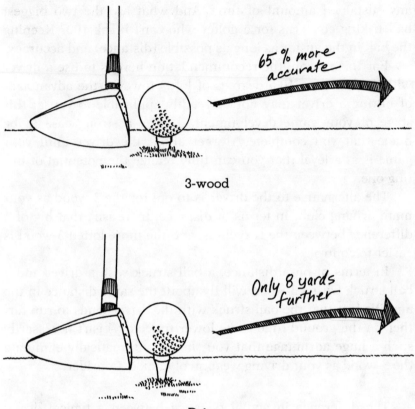

65 % more
accurate

3-wood

Only 8 yards
further

Driver

It's silly for the high handicap golfer to hit the driver from the tee.
He gains only eight yards in distance over the 3-wood, and
sacrifices much needed accuracy.

moving this fast at impact. When you combine the rate of
curve for a 3-wood with the typical width of a fairway, you
can see the odds are in your favor as far as keeping the ball
in the fairway.

• Since the distance differential between the driver and the 3-
wood occurs almost entirely on the ground, and since you're
less apt to hit the driver straight, chances are high that when

the ball struck with the driver hits the ground running it will be headed for trouble. That's not a good thing.

• You can make up some of the difference differential by installing a driver-length shaft into the 3-wood of your choice. The longer shaft will create a wider swing arc, more clubhead speed, and more power. The strong recommendation here is that for the course of this plan and perhaps for some time beyond, you abandon the driver and make the 3-wood your primary driving club.

YOU DON'T KNOW JACK—BUT YOU CAN THINK LIKE HIM

As previously noted, professional tour golfers have a huge influence on the average person's golf game. The tour players endorse certain types of equipment, and people buy that equipment. Tour players credit a swing technique or grip adjustment with their latest victory and the average guy is out on the range the next day trying the Big Winner's latest swing key.

Well, here's an endorsement of sorts for using the 3-wood as your primary driving club. Jack Nicklaus is perhaps, along with Greg Norman, the longest, consistently accurate driver the game has ever known. Did you know that Nicklaus frequently opts for his 3-wood more often in the course of his round than he does for his driver? Did you also know that players such as Davis Love III, Fred Couples, and Norman do the same—frequently hitting the 3-wood more often than the driver? Right there you have proof that the distance differential between the two clubs is not so enormous that it will hinder your game. Need more proof? Two of the greatest players in history, Sam Snead and Byron Nelson, never used drivers. They hit something akin to a 2-wood, as has Paul Azinger for much of his competitive career.

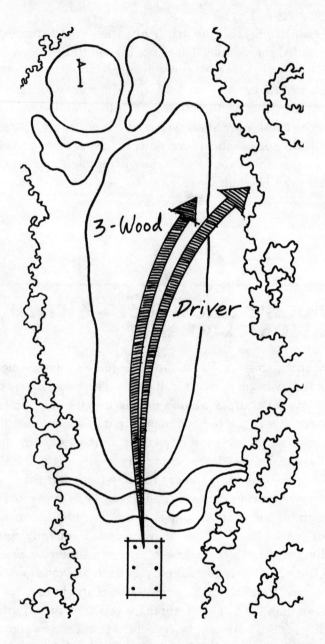

A 3-wood shot will curve off line less than a ball hit with the driver, so you have a much better chance of landing the 3-wood shot in the fairway—even when you mis-hit it.

Lose the Long Irons

There's no use beating around the bush about this point: You don't need long irons in your bag at this level of play. Very few golfers are capable of hitting a 2- or 3-iron, and even fewer are capable of hitting a 1-iron. You can automatically eliminate these clubs from your set makeup. The reason: The long irons, like the driver, have very little loft and, in general, present a tough visual image for most golfers, i.e., the ball isn't on a tee, the clubhead isn't all that big, and the player feels as if the chances of getting the ball airborne are slim. Also, since the long irons are best played with a "sweeping" motion, the likelihood of hitting the ball thin (with the lead edge of the clubface) is greatly increased.

The 4-iron is also a borderline club in this situation. The 7-wood is a better, easier-to-hit alternative to the 4-iron. If you think you might still need the 4-iron, keep track of how many times you use it over the course of five rounds. If it's among your least used clubs (and don't be surprised if it is) get rid of it. You should replace the long irons you remove from your set with a 5-wood, a 7-wood, and possibly even consider a 9-wood. If it makes you feel any better, the majority of players on the Senior PGA Tour and the LPGA Tour utilize 5-woods, 7-woods, and 9-woods rather than long irons. (LPGA Tour players Annika Sorenstam and Liselotte Neumann each carry an 11-wood.) The reason for choosing these clubs is simple. They are easier to hit than the long irons from any lie—from the rough, from a divot, off the tee. They also produce shots that fly higher and straighter (because they have more loft, which creates more backspin and less sidespin) and land softer, making it easier to keep your ball on the green on approach shots.

The L-wedge and Beyond

If you've decided to banish the 4-iron and haven't opted for the 9-wood, your set makeup at this point is as follows: 3-wood, 5-wood, 7-wood, and 5–9 irons, for a total of 8 clubs. The Rules of Golf allow you 14 clubs. You definitely need a putter, which will bring your total to 9 clubs. What should you do with the remaining choices? Think wedges. Add a pitching wedge and a standard sand wedge (that's 11 clubs) and perhaps, according to your feel, a 60-degree wedge and maybe even a 64-degree wedge.

Why so many wedges? Remember that 70 percent of your shots are hit from within 100 yards of the green. One of the toughest things for golfers of any level is to play shots that require a club to be hit less than its full distance. Another trying situation for the average golfer is when a short shot must be played high in the air to carry a hazard and then land softly on the green. The full complement of wedges allows you to play almost any shot without making adjustments in your swing. The 60-degree wedge can allow you to play short approach shots while still swinging fully through the ball, and the 64-degree wedge will allow you to pop the ball up and over bunkers without blinking. Just grab the club out of the bag and swing at it.

Even if you decide to carry all four wedges, your total is only up to 13. So now you can go back and decide on the 4-iron or the 9-wood. Check them out and see which one seems best for you.

Don't Get Shafted by Your Shafts

Today the average golfer is much more aware of the impact the shaft of the club has on the shots struck with the club—more so than in days gone by, at least. Still, it's a safe bet that more golfers have the wrong shafts in their clubs than have the correct ones. The reasons for this vary from ignorance to the simple fact that a lot of players use clubs that are hand-me-downs—clubs previously owned by and intended for use by a completely different individual. Having the correct type of shaft is important, because it's the shaft that connects your swing to the clubhead. A shaft that matches your strength and flexibility will allow you to create the most powerful shots. A shaft that doesn't match your strength and flexibility will result in shots that fly shorter than that of which you are capable, and just as assuredly, shots that are off target.

The biggest factor in determining the performance of a shaft is a property called flex. Since the shaft of a club is so thin, it bends and bows during the golf swing. The fact that it bends and bows (or flexes) is okay. The key is matching up a shaft with the correct amount of flex to the speed at which you swing the club. In general, the more speed created in your swing, the less flex you'll need. Note that the key here is how much speed you generate in your swing—not how strong you are. The physics of the golf swing allow some people who aren't very strong to generate amazing clubhead speed, so don't get caught up in the idea that clubhead speed is the result of brute strength.

So how do you determine which shaft flex is best for you? For starters you must bear this in mind: The measurement of the degree of flex in a shaft varies from manufacturer to manufacturer—there are no standards. So you have to judge each shaft based on its own merits and versus the same type of shaft from the same manufacturer.

Having said that, here's the first rule of choosing the shaft flex that's proper for you: You should swing the most flexible shaft you can possibly use without having an adverse effect on your shot patterns. This is contrary to the long-held convention that every golfer should use the stiffest possible shaft. Here's the reason why: The more flexible the shaft is, the more potential energy generated, stored, and released into the golf ball—which means more distance. The safest way to know for sure that you have the proper shaft flex in your clubs is to check with a PGA professional. However, a few telltale warning signs are listed below to help you stay alert to a mismatch between your shafts and you.

Stiff Punishment

The most common mistake the average golfer makes in selecting a shaft is choosing one that is too stiff. Sadly, a great number of these ill-fitting shafts are the result of the average guy's macho instinct to prove (mostly to himself) that he is strong like a bull. Well, here's a hot tip for you, Hercules: If the shafts of your clubs are too stiff, you'll end up with a whole bunch of problems. First off, your brain will sense that you are going to have trouble getting the ball into the air, and as such, it (your brain) will hit the appropriate panic buttons. "You'd better scoop this one into the air, dummy," says your brain. So you attempt to do just that, and you hang back on your right foot in the downswing, never shifting your weight through the ball, never turning your body through the ball. Anytime you see someone who finishes their swing with their weight on their back foot instead of their front foot, it's a pretty good bet the shafts in their clubs are too stiff.

When you hang on your back foot instead of turning through the ball you're capable of a variety of nasty things. Since the club will be moving into the ball at far too steep an angle, you're about equally likely to top the ball or to slam the club into the ground behind the ball. If you're lucky enough to make solid contact with the ball with a shaft that is too stiff, it's likely the ball will fly low and left of your target.

While it is very common to see players with shafts that are too stiff, it is much less so regarding shafts that are not stiff enough (commonly referred to as too weak or too soft). However, it does occur, and the giveaways that your shafts may too weak are quick, darting right-to-left shots (snap hooks) and high floaters that hang out to the right of your target.

True Lies

The angle at which the shaft of your club protrudes from the clubhead when the bottom of the club is flat on the ground is known as the lie of the club. The lie angle of your clubs is another critical factor in how well the clubs perform for you. The biggest factors in determining the proper lie angle is your physical height and the way you address the ball. Once again, a qualified clubfitter could tell you in a matter of minutes whether the lie of your clubs is right for you. Here's a few tip-offs that the lie of your clubs may be off the mark:

- If you pull a lot of shots to the left of your target—i.e., the ball flies on a straight line but that straight line happens to point left of your target—the lie angle of your clubs may be too steep, or too "upright." Clubs that are too upright will cause you to develop an unintended "chicken wing" with the left arm in the downswing. This prevents you from getting full extension through the ball.

- If the lie angle of your clubs isn't steep enough (too "flat"), you can make a perfect swing and still hit the ball out to the right on a straight line (a "push"). This can be bad news, since the natural instinct to correct this ball flight pattern would be to swing "over the top," or to loop the club at the top of your backswing, throwing it off plane and creating one of golf's true death moves.

If you're not convinced of the importance of proper lies, try this on for size: LPGA star Michelle McGann was struggling with leaving all of her iron shots out to the right of her target. She thought it was a swing problem and came to us for help. We checked the lies of her clubs and discovered they were too flat. As soon as the lies were adjusted, she started hitting them straight again.

Get a Grip

One element of proper clubfitting that is frequently overlooked is the rubber or leather grip on the end of the club, the fit of which depends solely on the size of your hands. A lot of golfers don't realize these grips come in various sizes—they think all grips are the same size. You, of course, aren't that stupid, but for the sake of thoroughness, here's a few pointers on making sure you have the right size grip on your club:

- If the grip is the correct size, the tips of your fingers should barely touch the palms of your hands when you're holding the club.

- If the grip on your club is too thick, it will increase the amount of tension it takes to hold the club (a bad thing), it will slow down your swing (a bad thing), and you will hit a lot of shots dead right of your target (a bad thing) because your wrists won't properly cock and uncock.

- If the grip on your club is too thin, it will cause your hands to be overactive, which will lead to an early release of the club and some low screaming hooks and pulls.

(Club)Head Games

Your quest to break 100 is significantly easier today than it would have been 30 years ago or so, when Karsten Solheim (the guy who invented Ping golf clubs) first conceived the idea of perimeter-weighted irons. Today, offset, perimeter-weighted, cavity back irons are the standard iron design, and it's almost unthinkable that you'd be playing something else unless you're playing with a set you got out of Uncle Bob's garage after he died. If you're not playing a perimeter-weighted iron, you should be. The offset on these clubs (the design feature that places the lead edge a bit behind the shaft) allows you to get the ball into the air easier and to get the clubface turning closed through impact. The latter helps you hit the ball from right to left, a ball flight that achieves maximum distance.

The perimeter-weighted design also produces more consistent shots, since nearly the entire clubface serves as a "sweet spot," the term used to describe the dime-size area on the old forged irons that needed to strike the ball to produce a good shot. Finally, perimeter-weighting makes even your real stinkers somewhat less stinky—you pretty much have to whiff to produce a shot completely lacking in merit.

Metal woods haven't been an equipment mainstay as long as perimeter-weighted irons (although they date back to the early part of the 20th century), but they accomplish the same thing: Namely, they allow your good swings to produce great results and your bad swings to produce results you can live with. The newer generation metal woods with huge clubheads, combined with a graphite shaft, are simply the easiest clubs to hit in the history of the game. If you can afford it, go big and go titanium as it relates to the clubhead in your woods, and go graphite in the shaft.

Close the Gaps

A typical set of irons is manufactured so that the lofts on the clubs will produce a consistent distance differential between each club, i.e., the properly struck 8-iron produces a shot that flies 10 yards farther than the properly struck 9-iron, the properly struck 7-iron produces a shot that flies 10 yards farther than the properly struck 8-iron, and so on. It is possible that, depending upon the quality and manufacturing of your clubs, the distance gaps between the clubs may not be consistent. You should check to make certain that they are, because it's essential that your set of irons provides you with consistent distances so that when you become more aware of course management you can make intelligent club selections. How can you do this? The most obvious way is to do it at a driving range either very early in the morning or late in the day, when it would be possible for you to hit 10 or so balls with each iron you carry and then walk out onto the range and check the yardage between the groups. This, of course, assumes you hit the balls in the same general vicinity. Don't count any balls that are obviously mis-hit.

Another way to check the gapping on your clubs would simply be to have a PGA pro or clubfitter check your loft angles on a loft and lie device. It's fairly simple, and it's doubtful they would charge you for it.

A Ball Is a Ball Is a Ball. Or Is It?

For almost everyone reading this book for its intended purpose, getting maximum distance out of your shots is a primary concern. This is especially true from the tee on driving holes. You've almost assuredly heard, seen, and/or read many of the claims golf ball manufacturers make regarding their products. Is any one brand of golf ball significantly longer than the rest? Not really—not, at least, if the ball is legal by the standards of the United States Golf Association.

However, there are two basic types of golf balls: the two-piece ball and the three-piece (or wound or soft) ball. In almost every case for the reader of this book, the two-piece, solid ball is the best option for a number of reasons, but here are the three main ones:

It flies farther in the air (1), and it rolls farther on the ground (2). The reason for this is that the ball doesn't spin as much as its three-piece brother, so it doesn't encounter as much wind resistance and it hits the ground running. The third reason is that balls of this type are, for all intents, indestructible.

Opting for this type of ball leaves you a little vulnerable hitting into the greens and around the greens, because this type of ball does generate a tremendous amount of spin to hold the ball on the green. There are two things you can do to greatly improve your chances around the greens. The first is to carry more lofted woods (5-, 7-, 9-woods) to hit into the greens, and to carry a 64-degree wedge. This won't put any extra spin on the ball, but it will create shots that come into the green at such a steep angle (dropping almost perpendicular to the putting surface) that the ball won't roll much at all once it lands on the green. You should take this tip as an absolute rule if you play a lot of golf at courses that have Bermuda rough. You'll have no chance of stopping this type of ball from Bermuda rough otherwise.

The second thing you can do is to play irons with square or U-shaped grooves etched into the clubface. Nearly every modern perimeter-weighted design has this type of groove, which, for some reason, imparts more spin on the ball than the classic V-shaped groove. Once a widely debated point, it is now generally accepted as fact that square or U-shaped grooves provide more spin than V-grooves.

To avoid confusion be aware that the two-piece ball is also referred to as a hard ball, a solid ball, a hot ball (although not in the illegal sense), a surlyn ball (although there are three-piece surlyn balls as well—surlyn is a cover material), and a rock.

The alternative to the two-piece ball is the three-piece ball. Also known as a wound ball (because it has rubber bands wound tightly around a tiny rubber ball at the core), a soft ball (because the cover feels softer than that of a two-piece ball), and a balata ball (because this type of ball was originally covered in a substance derived from balata trees), the three-piece ball is not a very practical alternative for someone whose game is at the level at which you currently find yourself. However, once your game gets to new levels, you may wish to consider a three-piece ball as your primary ball for two reasons: It offers greater maneuverability from side to side while in flight, and it is much more likely to hold the green once it hits the green.

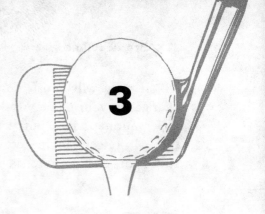

3

The Short Road to Success

When you have completed any necessary alterations to your equipment or juggled the elements that make up your set of clubs, you have completed the simplest phase of your journey to shatter 100. You didn't have to adjust the way you think, and you didn't have to make any physical changes in the way you swing the club—you just looked in your bag, really. The simplicity of it was the very reason it was the first thing you did.

Now it is time to move on to the next step of your quest, which also happens to be the next rung in order of simplicity. This chapter will tell you how to improve your short game, the phase of the game that consists of any shot closer than roughly 100 yards from the hole. What makes the short game so simple? We didn't say it was simple; we just said it was *simpler* than a lot of other things in golf. However, the short game is an ideal place to begin the renovation of your game, because it is the area in which you will most quickly and readily observe positive changes in your game. More specifically, you'll start to see some lower numbers in a hurry. (We know you want to start hitting the ball longer off the tee, but trust us on this one—the short stuff is the best place to start.)

The Short and the Short of It, or Get Shorty

Estimates vary on precisely how many shots the typical golfer plays from 100 yards and closer to the hole, but you can safely assume that if you're having trouble breaking 100, at least 60 percent of your shots are in this range. And because the short game is, well, short, there are a few built-in advantages. First, because the shots are intended to travel relatively short distances, the swings and/or strokes used to play them are, by nature, more economical in terms of movement and the length of time it takes to complete them. These two things add up to less room and time for errors to occur. The second built-in advantage to the short game is that because the shots are of a shortish nature, it is easier for you to judge them and to use whatever athletic instincts you possess. It is not a coincidence that putting is the area of the game where conforming to accepted mechanical standards matters least. There is more room for individuality in putting strokes because there are fewer ways you can screw it up—the shots are the shortest you play and the swing is the shortest you use. Less room for error.

Despite the fact that the short game is generally considered to consist of shots from 100 yards in, we're going to zoom in even closer to the hole and improve your game in the area directly surrounding the green, approximately a 40-yard diameter around the hole. You should approach all shots from within this zone with the same thing in mind: namely, you want the ball to be on the ground as much as possible. We realize it's not always possible to play the ball along the ground, but you should do so whenever you can. Rule number one of the short game, then, goes something like this: *minimum air time, maximum ground time*. Another way of looking at it might be in terms of football and one of its time-tested tenets: You have to establish

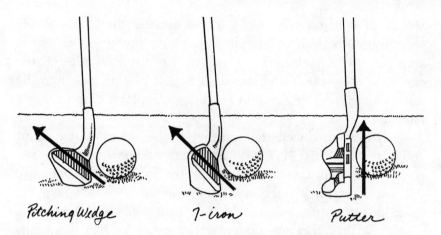

Pitching Wedge   *7-iron*   *Putter*

From right to left, the preferred methods of attack: putting, chipping, and pitching. Less lofted clubs such as the putter and 7-iron make it easier to get the ball rolling along the ground.

the ground game before you can open up the other phases of your offense. In your case, you have to establish the ground game around the green before moving on to other areas of your offense.

To become master of the zone that spreads out 40 yards in diameter from the hole, you have to become proficient at four shots: the long/lag putt, the basic chip, the basic pitch, and the garden-variety sand shot. You should learn them in that order as well, because rule number two of your new short game is: *Putt the ball whenever you can, even if you're not on the green. When you can't putt, chip. When you can't chip, pitch.*

The Ifs and Ands of Putts

There's a whole bunch of reasons why your putter should become your new best friend in your quest for short game improvement. The stroke required to use it has the least number of moving parts (less room for error) and also relies more on your natural instincts (such as judging distance and hand/eye coordination) than any other phase of the game. More importantly, a putt keeps the ball on the ground, where there is a lesser chance of it being affected by a bad bounce, the wind, or any sudden brain spasm you might have while attempting to play a chip shot. The likelihood of you sticking the lead edge of the club into the ground and chunking a putt are far less than the same scenario coming true in an attempt to play a chip shot or a pitch shot.

Still not convinced that putting is the easiest thing about golf? Consider this: Have you ever seen or known anyone that couldn't play miniature golf? It's pretty unlikely—the odds are that even the most uncoordinated individual would grasp the basic idea of putting and be able to execute the stroke and make contact with sufficient solidness to propel the ball along the ground in the general direction of his or her target. The same cannot be said of any other area of golf, not even the seemingly simple chip shot.

Since you're going to be relying so heavily on your putter, the first step toward improving this phase of your game is determining what sorts of things you should be doing in your stroke and strategy to allow you to first become a better long (lag) putter and, secondly, to become a better-than-average short putter.

TO PUTT OR NOT TO PUTT

You should always putt when. . .

. . . your ball is on the green, or on the fringe and the area between your ball and the hole is relatively flat. This assumes that the fringe is short and consistent in its length.

. . . your ball is sitting on the fairway in front of and within 5 yards of the green and you have an unobstructed path to the hole (including any dramatic changes in terrain, particularly uphill). This again assumes that the grass is of a length and consistency that the ball can roll along the ground without suddenly stopping dead in its tracks.

. . . you have a complete lack of confidence in your chipping game.

You should *probably* putt when. . .

. . . you feel you have a choice between a putt and a chip shot (this generally means there is very little or no rough between the ball and the hole), and the lofted shot would have to be played a "perfect" distance to leave your ball anywhere near the hole. In other words, if the green has a very distinct tier and the hole is cut to one side or the other of that tier, you'll want to play the ball along the ground with your putter; it is significantly easier to judge the distance of a putt than it is to accurately play a shot of a precise distance with a lofted club—at least at the level at which you currently play the game. As you improve, you may or may not reconsider this strategy. At the moment, however, it is your best bet.

You should never putt when. . .

. . . there's more than 12 inches of rough between your ball and the fringe of the green.

. . . there is any severely bumpy ground and clumpy grass between your ball and the green.

. . . there is a change of elevation between the fairway and green.

. . . there is a dramatic change of elevation on the green itself.

. . . it just seems too long to putt. If you have 80 feet to the hole, you're going to end up using a stroke that's too long for a putter and possibly bring some sidespin into the equation.

YOU, YOUR PUTTING STYLE, AND YOUR PUTTER

There's no question that of all the various movements and swinging motions in golf, putting allows the most room for individual traits and quirks. That's one of the main reasons that it's the phase of the game at which it is easiest to achieve a state that resembles proficiency. Having said that, however, you should keep in mind that there are some basic things you should do to increase the rate at which you improve (such as not putting the ball between your legs).

Before we hit you with some basics, however, you should know a basic that precedes all other basics: You have to determine which side is your dominant side in your putting stroke—your right or your left. This doesn't have anything to do with whether you putt right-handed or left-handed. Rather, it's about which arm has more control of your putting stroke. It truly is an overlooked "super basic"—something many players neglect or have never even considered. However, it influences everything else in your putting game, so let's look at how you determine which side is the most dominant in your putting stroke.

DO THE DRILL, HONE YOUR SKILL

Here's a simple drill you can do to determine which arm is the dominant arm in your putting stroke: Hit about 10 putts with just your right hand holding the putter; then hit about 10 putts with only your left hand holding the putter. The dominant side will feel fairly solid to you, and you won't have any trouble controlling the clubhead, that is to say, keeping it square. The non-dominant side (or for the sake of simplicity, the wrong side) will feel as if you must struggle with the clubhead to keep it square, and the putts going in the direction you aim them. You have to admit, that's pretty simple. Once you know which side is your dominant side, here's what you do with that information:

IF YOU'RE A LEFT-ARM–DOMINANT PUTTER...

. . . your left armpit should act as the "center" of your putting stroke.

. . . you should use a heel-shafted putter, the type of blade used by players such as Ben Crenshaw. This type of putter is designed to swing open and closed like a gate when being stroked, which is exactly what you need when you're a left-arm–dominant putter. (Be careful when selecting a putter based on this idea. Some perimeter-weighted putter designs join the shaft and hosel near the heel of the club, but the hosel actually attaches to the clubhead more toward the center.)

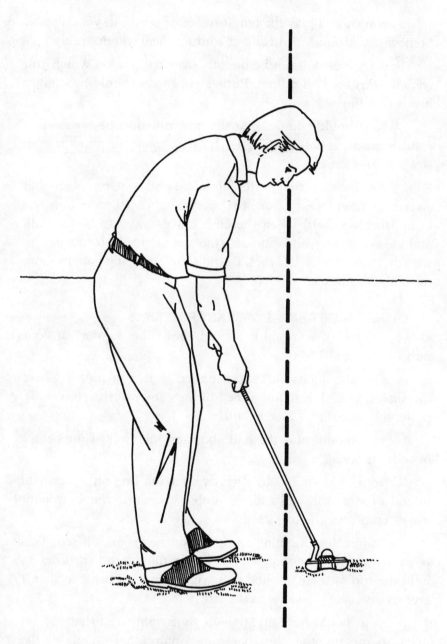

Left-arm–dominant putters should use heel-shafted putters and keep their eyes inside the line on which they want the ball to travel.

. . . you should play the ball forward of center in your stance. Somewhere around the inside of your left heel will do nicely.

. . . your eyes will not be directly over the line on which you wish to start the ball rolling. Rather, your eyes should be slightly inside that line.

. . . you should stand tall at the ball, not slouched over. As a result your arms will hanging fairly straight—loose, but straight. Not stiff and tense.

. . . the face of the putter should subtly swing open and closed (as mentioned before). It opens slightly (the toe fans out away from the ball) when the club moves away from the ball, and closes slightly after impact (the toe of the club turning in, slightly, toward your left toe). Despite this swinging gate motion, the club is square at impact.

IF YOU'RE A RIGHT-ARM–DOMINANT PUTTER. . .

. . . the top of your spine should act as the "center" of your putting stroke.

. . . you should use a center-shafted putter (a putter where the shaft and clubhead are joined in the center of the clubhead), preferably one that is face balanced.

. . . you should play the ball about an inch left of the center of your stance.

. . . your eyes should be directly over the line on which you intend to start the ball rolling, preferably with your dominant eye directly over the ball itself.

. . . rather than hanging straight, your arms are angled. This is based on the fact that your left arm must bend in order to hold the top of the club, and your right arm will bend so that it creates an angle the same as the left.

. . . you should have an angle in your right wrist that you set prior to moving the club back and maintain throughout the entire stroke. Very roughly speaking, this angle ranges from 45 to 90 degrees, depending upon the player.

. . . the clubhead moves away from the ball on a straight line and returns through the ball on the same line. There is no devia-

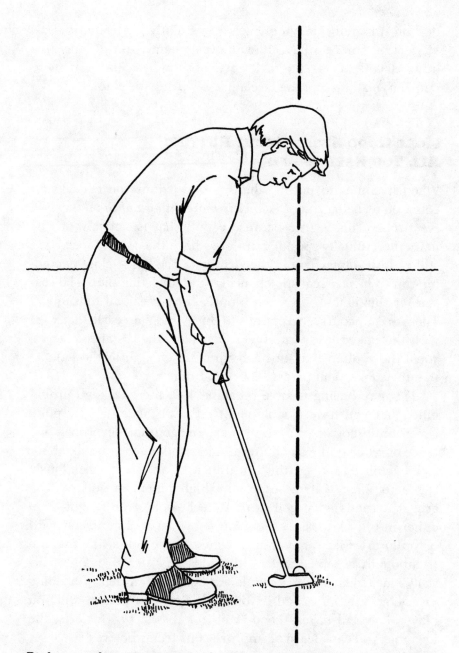

Right-arm–dominant putters should use center-shafted putters and keep their eyes directly over the line on which they want the ball to travel.

tion on this point on short putts. On slightly longer putts—say, 15 feet or more—the putter moves slightly inside the line (toward you). Don't try to keep it absolutely square on these putts or you'll disrupt the face angle by lifting the club.

More Good Stuff About Putting: All You Need Is Lag

When it comes to putting, here is one axiom you can always count on as being true: *Distance is more important than direction every time.* This is true because a putt that is horribly off the mark directionally speaking but does have the correct speed will still end up somewhere in the vicinity of the hole—close enough for you to have a realistic chance at the following putt. The reason for this is that, in general, putts don't break all that much. There are, of course, exceptions to this, which are easily detected with the naked eye. However, if you have the distance correct, you'll more often than not end up close enough to the hole so that the subsequent putt will be a no-brainer.

If you're having trouble breaking 100, there's a high probability that you have trouble getting the distance of your putts consistently correct. To a large extent, getting the proper distance on your putts is a matter of feel. And when you talk about feel in golf, you're getting into an area that is tremendously vague to most golfers—especially high handicap golfers. The accepted thinking in golf is that "feel" cannot be taught—you either intuitively possess feel (you've always had it, always will) or you don't. Like many things related to the golf swing that are traditionally accepted as fact, this idea about "feel" is only partially true. Indeed, some people are born with a "feel" for doing just about anything, and if you're that type of person and you play golf, you'll have a good "feel" for the game. However, the idea that you can't learn to improve your feel is hogwash.

Here's another truth about the distance factor of your putts: The longer a putt is, the more difficult it is to roll the ball the correct distance. Since you're having trouble cracking 100, two things can be safely assumed about your putting: You don't hit the ball all that close to the hole, so you have a lot of long putts;

and you don't get your long putts very close to the hole.

The art of getting your long putts close to the hole is, as you may know, referred to as lagging the ball. It's a rather weak-sounding word for such an important element of your game, but the intent of a lag putt is to focus on getting the ball close to the hole rather than actually holing the ball. "Lag" refers to the idea of holding back on the stroke so as to not get overly aggressive.

Here's some good news for you: You can learn to get your long putts close to the hole. Keep reading, because we're going to tell you exactly how to do it.

THE LONGEST SHORT ROAD HOME

The single biggest reason for having difficulty getting the ball close to the hole on long putts is this: You don't practice them. Think about it. You go to the practice green, and you drop a few balls on the green. You pick a hole and hit the balls at it. You pick another hole and hit the balls at it. The target holes you select are generally close to you. And then before you dash off to the first tee you might hit one or two long putts. (We say dash off to the first tee because the only time you practice your putting is during the 10 minutes before you tee off, right?)

So here's your first tip: We know you spend all of whatever practice time you have smashing balls with your driver and irons. Spend some of your time on the practice green, and spend most of that time working on putts of 35 feet or longer. Sound boring and a little less fun than crushing balls with your driver? If you want to break 100, it's just as important to practice your long putting. When you start out you don't need to have any specific thoughts or goals. Just by practicing longer putts you'll be exercising your mind and body at becoming familiar with the "feel" necessary to be proficient on long putts.

PRETEND YOU'RE AT THE ALLEY, CAT

Nearly anything that can modestly be described as an athletic endeavor requires a bit of basic hand-to-eye coordination. One

When facing a long putt, imagine yourself rolling the ball to the hole with your dominant arm. The distance you move your arm is approximately the distance your putter should move for a putt of that length.

of the most basic skills, athletic or not, is being able to determine how hard you would have to throw an object for it to travel a certain distance. Think about it this way: If you were 10 feet away from someone and you were tossing a ball back and forth, you wouldn't have to think about how hard to toss the ball, would you? You would simply look at the person, your arm would move, and the ball would almost certainly be propelled with the correct amount of force to reach the hands of the person with whom you're playing catch.

Another sensation that most people share is this: If someone gave you a smallish ball (a tennis ball, for example) and told you to roll it along the ground to a target, you would probably roll the ball fairly close to the target without giving it much thought. So here's the point (and your tip): The next time you have a long putt, stand next to the ball and visualize yourself in a bowling alley. Gently move your dominant arm (which you've already determined) slowly back and forth while looking at the hole, and determine how far you would have to swing your arm back and forth to roll the ball toward the hole—the hole representing the bowling pins in this example. Some of the very best players in the world do this from time to time, not the least of whom is Nick Faldo, the best player of his era. You'll notice that your arm moves back and through the same distance. That's exactly the same distance your arm should swing back and forth for a putt of that distance. The key here is to be certain that your arm (and your entire body) is relaxed. And keep this in mind: Your arms always move the same distance back and through the ball.

KEEP YOUR EYE ON THE HOLE. (HAH! YOU THOUGHT WE WERE GOING TO SAY "BALL," DIDN'T YOU?) PLUS MORE COOL TIPS

If it's not already a basic part of your preparation to hit a putt, you should incorporate a few practice strokes (two or three quick ones will do it) into your routine on the greens. The good part of your practice strokes is that you can do a bunch of good things in a few seconds—much more than you can in the same amount of time applied to any other phase of your game.

Here's Good Thing No. 1:

By looking at the hole—not at the ball—when you take your practice strokes, you can help ingrain the "bowling alley" feeling described above. Your eyes and your brain are your most valuable tools in golf, so use 'em. And more importantly, trust them. When you look at the hole while you take your practice strokes, you are subconsciously programming your body to hit the ball with the proper force. Just repeat that stroke when you actually hit the putt.

Good Thing No. 2:

Since distance is such an important part of putting, wouldn't it be nice if there were more ways to get a feel for the distance with your practice strokes? Putting allows you a chance to do this. Here's how: When you have a putt that will travel along mostly level portions of the green, you should take your practice strokes from right next to the ball—but you shouldn't take your practice strokes from right next to the ball on every putt. When you have an uphill putt, take your practice strokes farther from the hole than the ball's actual location—how far depends upon how steep a hill your ball has to climb. (The only way to determine how far is to just start doing it and figure it out for yourself.) Now, when you're taking those practice strokes farther from the hole, you're trying to determine how hard you would hit a putt *over flat terrain from the exaggerated distance*. Once again you'll be using your trusty eyes and brain, and your new best friend, the "bowling alley move." Once you get a feel for how hard the stroke would be from the increased distance, move back to the ball and put the same stroke on it you were practicing from behind the ball.

Good Thing No. 3:

We were kind of hoping you'd figure this one out on your own, but here it is: Just as you took your practice strokes from behind the ball on uphill putts, you should take your practice strokes closer to the hole (in front of the ball) on downhill putts. Once again, how far ahead of the ball you stand depends on the severity of the slope, and you should also visualize a flat putt from the point closer to the hole. This will help you get the feel for the proper length stroke you need to put on the ball.

PICK A DOT, THEN HIT THAT SPOT

While distance is your primary consideration on the greens, you need to give some consideration to the possibility that the ball may not roll directly toward the hole. The line along which a putt—especially a long putt—must travel has to be given some consideration. If you were asked to guess how often you face a dead straight putt in golf, what would your answer be? Half the time? It's nearly impossible to assign a definite percentage to this answer, but the fact is that you rarely face a *dead straight* putt, because greens are not generally constructed perfectly flat. If they were, there wouldn't be any place for the water to run off when it rains.

You have to be fairly close to the hole for the ball to run on a dead line to the hole. It happens, of course, just as once in a while you'll have a long putt that runs straight to the naked eye. The odds are excellent that any putt you make will curve along the ground in one direction or the other, and the likelihood that this will occur and the amount of the curve both increase as the ball moves farther and farther from the hole. In other words, generally speaking, the longer a putt is, the more it's going to break than a shorter putt on the same line. This is a crucial point to consider in getting your long putts close to the hole, because the farther you are from the hole, the more difficult it is for you to get your body and the clubface properly oriented in relation to the hole. Why? *Because there is a tendency to regard the hole as your aiming point. The hole is not your aiming point unless you have a dead straight putt.* The hole is your target in the sense that it is where you want your ball to end up, but don't confuse the words "target" and "aiming point."

Before this gets too confusing, let's digress for a moment. Despite the fact that the hole is the eventual target in golf, it is not the target for most of the shots you play. Typically, you are too far away from it to see the actual hole in the ground. This is why golfers commonly aim their body and/or their clubface at the hole even though they both should be aimed at the line along which you wish the ball to start. Because you can make visual contact with the hole, however, there is a tendency to "cheat" and aim the clubface at the hole, or "steer" the clubface toward the hole after contact with the ball, which leads to an off-line putt.

So the two basic problems are as follows: On a long putt there's a good chance the putt is going to break, perhaps a significant amount; and it's difficult to get your body and the putter properly aimed due to the proximity of the prey you stalk—the wily hole in the ground.

Here's how you solve these two problems: First, make a determination as to how much you think the ground is going to affect the ball, forcing it to move. Keep in mind that the length of the putt and the speed at which the ball will be traveling are two key things to consider. (The main thing to consider, of course, is the terrain itself.) The faster the ball is moving, the less it will break. The slower it is moving, the more it will break. It follows, then, that the ball is moving fastest when you first strike it, so the terrain won't affect it as much there as it does when the ball is moving slower, i.e., nearer the hole.

The next step is to pick a line along which you want to start your putt rolling. Pick a spot on the ground along that line between two and eight inches from the ball. Use your imagination; zoom in on a blade of grass that is a slightly different color, an old ball mark, a spike mark, a granule of sand—anything. Now aim your putter at that spot, and align your body parallel to the line along which you've aimed: Your feet, shoulders, eyes, should all be parallel to that line. Now hit the putt, with this one single thought in mind: *Keep the clubface moving directly toward the spot. Do not shove it toward the hole.* It's simple. You keep the clubface moving toward the spot and the putt will start on line. You move the clubface toward the hole and your putt has no chance of staying on line—in fact, it will be off-line the second you strike it.

BASKET SCHMASKET—GET THE BALL REAL CLOSE

There are copious amounts of visualization techniques and metaphors in golf, all of which are intended to help the average golfer improve his performance. Some have been repeated for years on end and are thought to be solid bits of advice simply for that reason. Here's the classic tip that relates to "lag" putting: Imagine a huge circle or basket around the hole—extending out in a three-foot circumference from the hole—and simply try to get your putt somewhere within this circle. Don't worry about trying to get the ball in the hole; anywhere in the circle will do just fine. Here's our assessment of this tip: It stinks. You should be concentrating on *narrowing* your focus, not widening it. In fact, "focus" in the mental sense means to be very precise about what you're trying to achieve.

The point of the "big basket" tip is that it is somewhat overwhelming to aim at a target as small as the hole—that you are incapable of judging how hard to hit the ball to get it close to the hole. Somehow, the logic goes, you will feel more comfortable if the size of your "landing zone" is bigger. Do you buy that? Do you really think you're any less capable of getting the ball to within three feet of the hole than you are of getting it close enough to tap it in? Of course not—it's a silly tip. Besides, a three-foot putt is no guarantee. And what if you miss the basket? If you're so unsure of yourself that you're aiming for that huge circle, what's your state of mind going to be if you miss the circle? That five-footer you have left is going to look like a mile.

Your best bet is to narrow your focus, and try to get the ball as close to the hole as you possibly can. Trust us—if you can get it within three feet, you're more often than not just as capable of getting it close enough to tap it in without giving it much thought. To do this, concentrate on rolling the ball over a spot as previously described.

THE MOST COMMON ERROR ON LONG PUTTS

The biggest problem people have with long putts is not so much an error as it is a characteristic: They simply can't get comfortable with long putts. We've already discussed the biggest thing you can do to eradicate this problem—simply spend more time practicing long putts on the practice green.

However, the mechanical breakdowns that result from a lack of feel and confidence can be narrowed down to a single area on which you can concentrate. Once you've begun working on getting a feel for distance on putts, you'll want to combine that with a concerted effort to reduce the amount of excessive movement of the clubface and your body—the two almost always go together.

It's this simple: When you are putting, your arms are the only body parts that should be moving. (The only external body parts, anyway. We strongly advise that you continue to use any vital internal organs.) It is almost incomprehensible how some golfers get so many things moving when they are simply trying to roll the ball along the ground. We've seen players shift their weight like they are preparing to hit a drive, yank their arms upward as if they were anticipating a Nolan Ryan fastball, and then nearly top—yes, top!—a putt. And when you move your body, there's a good chance the clubface is going to be moving all over the place, too. When that happens the ball could be headed anywhere. Here's a "do" and "don't" list to help you stay steady over the ball:

DO...

. . . pinch your knees together a little bit, and maybe go for a bit of a pigeon-toed effect. Two of the very best putters of all time, Arnold Palmer and Jack Nicklaus, both did this to some degree. Nicklaus didn't go so much for the pigeon-toed look, but he definitely pinched in his knees. For the perfect example, find a picture of the youthful Arnold Palmer. You'll be able to feel the solid nature of this position simply by looking at him. In his heyday, Palmer was a rock over the ball on the putting green. Pinching your knees in this manner will force your weight to the inside of your feet. You'll immediately notice how anchored you feel to the ground. (The pigeon-toed look might make it a bit easier for you to bend your knees toward each other.)

. . . pretend there is a tack sticking out of the back of the ball, and try to drive that tack directly into the back of the ball. This mental image will remind you to keep the clubhead accelerating through the ball, which is one way of preventing the clubface from twisting open or closed through impact.

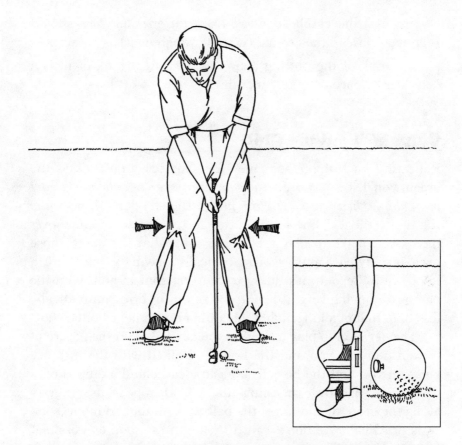

By driving the imaginary tack into the back of the ball, you will keep your clubhead accelerating through the ball, an essential element of good putting.

. . . pick a spot about two inches in front of the ball and concentrate on passing the clubhead directly over that spot. This is another way of ensuring that you keep the clubface square and accelerating through the ball.

DON'T. . .

. . . move your feet in any way, shape, or form. Keep 'em planted.

. . . shift your weight from one side to the other. Stay steady.

. . . "lift" the clubhead away from the ground. You should keep it as close to the ground (without touching it) as possible.

. . . think of the putting action as a swing. Think of it as a consistently paced stroke. Smooth.

Chips Without the Chili

Reflecting back upon our rules for shot selection around the green, you'll see they are: *Putt whenever you can; when you can't putt, chip; when you can't chip, pitch.* The standard chip shot is the first "fallback" line from putting for two reasons: The movements you make to play a chip are somewhat similar to those used in playing a putt—you're basically playing a putt with a lofted club. Second, it's the next simplest shot in golf, with the clubhead moving very little and the room for error dramatically less than that of a longer shot, including the standard pitch shot.

The decision to play a chip is typically based on the nature of terrain between you and the hole, combined with the distance between you and the hole. The basic idea behind a chip shot is to fly your ball over anything that would impede its progress along the ground, and to get the ball back on the ground as soon as is practical. (We don't want to tell you "as soon as possible" because that might not give you enough juice to get the ball to the hole.) Having said that, here's your chip shot checklist:

YOU SHOULD CHIP WHEN. . .

. . . you are within 5–20 yards from the front edge of the green, the approach (the area between you and the hole) is generally flat, and you do not perceive anything in the roll of the terrain or height of the grass that will hinder the progress of the ball. (Attempting to putt from this zone would most likely cause a breakdown in your stroke or leave the ball well short of the hole.) The ball can only travel so far along the ground when struck with a proper putting stroke, and traveling through more than a few yards of fairway-height grass takes too much speed off the ball.

. . . you are on the fringe and there is a clump of grass directly in your line to the hole, and this clump of grass will almost certainly throw the ball way off line and/or slow it down significantly. A *caveat* here: If you are very close to the hole in this situation and you think the amount of force necessary to clear the impediment will send the ball well past the hole, you might want to take your chances with a putt.

. . . there is three yards or less of rough between your ball and the edge of the green, and the ball is sitting up in the grass in a manner that will make it easy to get the club on the ball.

YOU SHOULD *PROBABLY* CHIP WHEN. . .

. . . the line between your ball and the hole is such that it forces any putt you might play to travel through an amount of fringe (four or five feet, perhaps) that is outside the bounds of your comfort zone.

. . . your ball is in front of the green and the green runs so severely uphill that a putt played to get to the hole would require a stroke the length of which would make it impossible to remain still over the ball. The chip allows you to play a shot of greater force with a shorter swing.

YOU SHOULD NEVER CHIP WHEN. . .

. . . there is more than three yards of rough between your ball and the edge of the green.

. . . the distance between your ball and the hole is so short that playing the shot with the force necessary to carry any impediment will send the ball rolling well beyond the hole— perhaps even farther away than you were to begin with.

. . . your ball is sitting so far down in the rough that you cannot see the bottom half of it, i.e., you're looking down and all you can see is the top of the ball.

. . . the greens and fairways are excessively wet, so any shot stops immediately upon landing.

PLAYING THE BASIC CHIP SHOT

Before you even begin to set up to play the standard chip shot, you have to determine which club you're going to use to play the shot. Typically you're only attempting to move the ball in the air a few feet—a couple of yards maximum. The other consideration is that you do need to both get the ball up in the air and then down on the green rather quickly. As a result, you can narrow your choices down to three irons. Played with a short, controlled stroke, your 5-iron, 7-iron, and 9-iron can be used for any chip shot.

The variance in the height of the shots created by these clubs when played with the shortish stroke required will produce shots of differing lengths. Which club do you use when? If the hole is on the far side of the green from you, it's the 5-iron. If the hole is in the center of the green, it's the 7-iron. If the hole is on the part of the green closest to you, it's the 9-iron. This eliminates any guesswork and indecision and allows you to concentrate on the shot.

What possible variables should you consider when selecting a club to play a standard chip? If you narrow it down to the 8-iron, 9-iron, and pitching wedge, the biggest consideration is the length of the clubs. If your clubs are properly matched, there should be a half-inch difference in length between them. As a result, the 9-iron is a half-inch shorter than the 8-iron; and the pitching wedge is a half-inch shorter than the 9-iron. It's not unusual for a player to feel more in control with a shorter club. (The putter is the shortest club in your bag, which is one of the reasons why you *should* feel in control of it.)

Of course, the loft of the club *is* a consideration, and as your game improves it will become even more of a consideration. However, as previously noted, the difference is negligible at this stage of your game. Select the one of these three clubs you're most comfortable with and stick with it. And remember: Minimum air time, maximum ground time. Don't get too carried away concerning yourself with how long the ball is going to stay in the air—just get it in the air long enough to carry whatever it is you're attempting to carry.

READY, SET, CHIP

The setup and stroke for playing a chip shot are similar to those required for putting, but there are some differences. Because your putting setup is a very individual thing, there isn't much point in making comparisons between the two. The single biggest communality is this: You want to be rock steady—no body movement except your arms—over a putt, and you want the same when playing a chip shot.

The basics for playing the standard chip shot are:

- **Open yourself up.** In your golf game, "open" has two different meanings. When your body is "open" it is aimed left of your target. When the club or clubface is said to be "open" it is aimed right of the target. When you're preparing to play a standard chip shot, you want your lower body to be "open" to the line on which you intend the ball to travel. In this sense, "open" means you want your feet and hips aimed slightly— emphasis on *slightly*—left of the target. The shoulders, however, should be square to the target line. This will allow the club to stay aimed at the target and move along the target line.

- **Play the ball back in your stance.** Most high handicap golfers feel compelled to help "lift" the ball into the air. This is particularly true in the short game. But what you might perceive as "helping" the ball into the air is detrimental, because it encourages excessive movement in your wrists. This frequently results in the shot being bladed with the lead edge of the club or the club digging into the ground too far behind the ball.

    There are a few things you can do to ensure clean contact with the ball when you're chipping. First, trust your equipment. The loft of the club will create the desired lift on the ball even *when you hit down on the ball*. This is important, because you most definitely want to *strike every chip shot with a descending blow*. The descending blow (the hitting down on the ball) eliminates the tendency toward overactive wrists.

The easiest way to make certain that you strike the ball while the club is traveling downward is to play the ball back in your stance. "Back" in this sense means more toward your right foot than your left foot. If you visually determine the center line between your feet, be certain to place the ball on the right side of that line. Exactly how far to the right of that line is effective is something you can determine by practicing, but for starters it's not a bad idea to split the difference.

- **Lean into the shot.** Another thing that will help you create a descending blow is to situate yourself so that you are leaning slightly toward your target. This happens rather naturally when you open your stance. Obviously, you don't wish to get yourself off balance, but you'll find it very helpful in doing two things. First, it will place your weight so that it favors the left leg, and this aids in hitting down on the ball. Second, it helps you become more oriented toward the target. A natural question is to wonder exactly how much of your weight should be tilting to the left. If you keep it in the 60–65 percent range you'll be just fine, and this is pretty easy to sense. You should feel solidly anchored with this much weight tilting toward the target—any more and you'd feel as if you were going to fall over, and with any less your weight wouldn't feel as if you were leaning at all.

- **Reach for it—just a little.** In almost every shot you play you'll be encouraged to have your arms hang freely and to feel loose and relaxed. This is one situation where you might want to try something a little different. Since the ball is back in your stance, you should feel as if your arms (and as a result, the club) are reaching back to the ball just a bit. It is quite important that you don't overdo this; however, it can be useful. This feeling of reaching just a tad will do two things: straighten (but not stiffen) your left arm, and set your right wrist at the proper angle. What is that angle? Here's a visualization technique for you: Imagine you're back in grade school (scary, isn't it?) and the teacher has called you to the blackboard. "Now Johnny," she says, "make a check mark."

Do that right now—make an imaginary check mark with your hand extended out in front of you. (Don't do it on a table as if you're writing; it's important that you do it in front of you.) When you finish making that check mark, hold that angle. That's the one you want in your right wrist as you prepare to play a chip shot.

- **Keep your eyes inside the line—slightly.** You've probably noticed that a lot of the things in this checklist include qualifying words such as "slightly" and "just a bit." Well, here's another one: Keep your eyes slightly inside your target line. This should happen fairly naturally, since the angle of the club will force you away from the ball slightly more than if you were putting. Just be careful not to get *too* far away from the ball. This can really have a negative impact on the perception of your relationship to the target that your eyes transmit to your brain. That's a bad thing.

- **Sometimes choking is a good thing.** Remember when we were chatting about putting? We said that one of the reasons it was easy to improve upon was that it was the shortest stroke and thus an easy stroke to control. Another reason it's easy to control the stroke is because the club itself, the putter, is easy to control. Why is that? Because it's the shortest club in the bag and therefore the least unwieldy of the bunch.

    The stroke for playing the basic chip shot is short as well, and you shouldn't be at all concerned with generating power. A chip shot is about control, so gain maximum control over the club by choking down as much as is practical on the club—to the point where it is almost putter length.

- **Do some toe-tapping.** Probably the single biggest misfire when attempting chip shots is getting the club stuck in the grass or stuck in the ground behind the ball. This happens for reasons too numerous to go into, and it's not necessary to know them. All you need to know is how to avoid this common screwup. And there is one way that's as close to surefire as you can get in golf: Stand the club on its toe for every chip shot. (The toe is the part of the clubhead that is the farthest away from you when you address the ball.)

Understanding why you are doing this will also help you determine to what extent you should do it, so here's the idea: By having only a minimal amount of the bottom of the club contact the ground, you greatly reduce the chances of the club getting snagged or stuck. The easiest way to minimize the amount of club-to-ground contact is to set only the part of the bottom out near the toe of the club on the ground.

Another way of thinking of this is that you are lifting the heel of the clubhead (the part closest to you) up off the ground. This is especially helpful when you are playing from long grass, since the heel is where the shaft joins the club-head, creating more mass for potential entanglement.

The easiest way to get a feel for this is to set the club on the ground as you would for a typical shot, with the sole of the club (the bottom of it) flush to the ground. Now tip the shaft of the club away from you, moving the shaft toward being perpendicular with the ground. That's the basic idea. It will look a little different as you're setting up to play a chip shot, because your hands will be ahead of the ball, but the basic thought is to lean the shaft away from your body. It's highly unlikely that you currently set the club this way, and it may feel a bit awkward at first—but there's no question that it will pay big dividends for you once you get comfortable with it.

The question of course is, to what extent do you lean the club away from you? The basic idea is to create space between the club and the ground, so the more you move the shaft toward vertical, the more space you create. You'll notice as you do this, however, that the tendency is for your hands to move forward to keep the lead edge of the club squared to the target. That's okay—you have to keep the lead edge aimed at the target, and moving your hands toward the target is yet another thing that helps ensure a descending blow. As your hands move forward, however, you are chang-ing the loft of the club, lessening it in effect. This is some-thing to consider when making your club selection, but it's not a huge factor, since tremendous height is not one of the qualities you seek in a chip shot. It should be a major consideration only if you favor lower-lofted clubs for chipping. Going back to the original question of how much should you lean the club, the answer is, at least enough to get the heel off the ground, but not so much that shaft actually becomes perpendicular to the ground, at about the same lie as your putter. If you stand the club up totally while choked down on it, the part that sticks out above your hands can get in the way of your stroke.

- **Think putt.** The similarities between a chip and a putt are numerous. To begin with, once the ball is in motion you want it to act as much like a putt as possible. To that end, playing the shot with the club on its toe offers the added bonus of a predictable reaction once you strike the ball. When you play the shot with the club in this position the ball comes off the clubface softer and is far less likely to "jump" or come off the clubface too hot.

  As for the stroke itself, it resembles the putting stroke quite a bit as well. Simply move your shoulders and arms back and forth, maintaining any angles you've set in your wrists and arms. Once you've properly taken care of the setup, the proper stroke will feel most natural to you.

  Other similarities between chipping and putting: It's not a bad idea to look at the hole while you make your practice strokes. Another part of the putting pre-shot routine that is very effective before chipping is to imagine how far you would move your arm back and forth if you were rolling the ball toward the hole. That's about how long your stroke should be. That should tell you something: How hard should you hit a chip shot? You should hit it with the same amount of force you would hit a putt of a similar distance.

COMMON MISTAKES

We mentioned above that the most common miscue in playing chip shots is hitting the ground behind the ball or getting the club entangled in the grass. While these are common results, they are just that—results. They aren't mistakes. Mistakes are the things that create poor results. Here are the most common mistakes in attempting to play a chip shot:

- **Playing the ball too far forward in your stance.** This goes back to that idea of trying to "help" the ball into the air. The thinking behind it goes something like this: If I play the ball forward in my stance, I'll catch it on the upswing and lift it into the air. The last thing you want to do is catch the ball once the club has started swinging up, because all that's going to happen is you're going to contact the ball with the edge of the club rather than the face of the club. Unless a ball is teed up, the only way to get the clubface on the ball is to hit down on it. The more to the left in your stance you position the ball, the more you increase the likelihood that you're going to catch the ball on the upswing—and that's a no-no. If you're catching a lot of your chip shots with the edge of the club and sending them way past your target, you should check whether you have the ball positioned too far forward.

- **You open your shoulders to the target, but forget about the other key body points.** It's not uncommon for people to confuse "open" with simply aiming the shoulders left of the target. If you remember, when we talked about "opening" your stance we referred to your entire body, or at least the key aiming points, which are your feet, knees, hips, and shoulders. Simply turning your shoulders to the left of the target isn't going to get the job done, regardless of the fact that the stroke is one of limited movement. If you aim your shoulders left of the target line and leave the rest of the key points square to the target line you will make it impossible for the clubface to remain square to your target. Rather, you've put yourself in a position that will cause the clubface to be closed (aimed left of the target) and moving on an in-to-out line when you contact the ball. The result is, you'll yank the ball left of the line you wanted it to start on.

- **You use a club with too much loft.** The chip shot at its essence is a running shot, meant to be played almost entirely along the ground. Under certain circumstances (i.e., from deep rough when the green is running severely away from you) you may want to play a chip shot that pops briefly into the air and lets a slope carry it away once it hits the ground. This is an exception, however. The setup, stroke, and club selection for playing a chip shot are based on the idea that the ball is going to be propelled predominantly forward (as opposed to up), and that this forward motion will be the primary fuel for the shot (as opposed to the terrain). As a result, if you take the chip setup and stroke and combine them with too much loft you will hit a dud—a shot that lands and only rolls a few inches (unless you get lucky and the terrain gives the ball added roll). So when playing your chip shots, leave any club with more loft than a pitching wedge in the bag.

- **You stand too far away from the ball.** When you stand too far away from the ball you have to extend your arms more than is advisable, and this creates a whole bunch of problems for you. First, when your arms are stiff it is very difficult to maintain any sense of feel for the clubhead. As your chipping improves you'll notice how important a role feel plays in the precision of your shots, so you don't want to do anything that will inhibit your feel.

    The second reason you don't want to stand too far from the ball is that, ideally, you want the path of the clubhead to go straight back from the ball and straight through the ball. If your arms are extended too much, the club will start to swing around you as opposed to straight back. Once the club starts to swing around you (swing open) it has to swing back again (swing closed) and the probability of it being square to the target is quite low. It would require an expert sense of timing to successfully chip with the club following this path.

Pitch a Perfect Game

So what exactly is the difference between a pitch and a chip? The two can be differentiated mainly by the amount of time the ball spends in the air and the height the ball reaches while it's in the air. Generally speaking (and we say this because in golf there are always exceptions), a chip is in the air for less time than a pitch and does not fly at as high a trajectory. The pitch flies higher and longer.

The pitch is, of course, the last of your three short game options over which you have any control. (The basic sand shot is part of your short game, but that decision is pretty much made for you.) To this point we've given you a list of situations in which you would choose to play either a putt or a chip, to help guide you through the thought process demanded by the rule: *Putt whenever you can, chip when you can't putt, and pitch when you can't chip.*

Here's guidelines for determining when you should pitch:

YOU SHOULD PITCH WHEN...

. . . the terrain or the height of the grass makes it impractical to putt or chip. Chipping becomes impractical when the distance that must be carried at the trajectory of a chip would require far too much force to be imparted upon the ball, i.e., it would send the ball rolling way, way past your target. As far as when it's impractical to putt, that should be fairly obvious: Whenever there's anything the ball can't roll through, over, or around, it's impractical to putt.

. . . you've got to carry any sort of other obstacle or hazard, namely a bunker or water hazard.

. . . the course is exceedingly wet and any shot played pretty much stays where it lands. In this scenario, you want to play the ball as close to the hole as possible on the fly.

THIS PITCH, THAT PITCH, OR THE OTHER PITCH

To make it in the major leagues they say a pitcher has to have at least three great pitches, the idea being that if he's only got one or two good ones there isn't enough in his repertoire to keep the world's best hitters guessing. In your quest to break 100 it helps to have three variations of the basic pitch shot (they don't have to be great ones) that you can consistently execute. (The good news is there aren't any line drives that come screaming back at your head after your pitches. See, golf really is a great game.)

The reason you should have the three different types at your disposal is that the scenarios under which you play a pitch shot are significantly more diverse than those under which you play a putt or a chip. The three types of pitch shots are one that *sits*, one that *walks*, and one that *runs*. The pitch that *sits* has the highest trajectory and rolls very little (just a few inches) once it lands on the green. The pitch that *walks* has a slightly lower trajectory than the sit pitch and rolls more once it hits the green. The pitch that *runs* has the lowest trajectory of the three and, as you might suspect given its name, runs quite a bit once it hits the green.

Before we talk about how to play each of the three types, the first thing you need to know is *when* you would play each of the shots.

Sit!

When you determine you want to land the ball as close to the hole as possible and have it stop, you want to play the sit pitch. Under what circumstances would you want the ball to stop its forward motion almost immediately? The most common situation that would require this shot is when there is very little green between you and the hole. The minimal amount of room makes it necessary, because if the ball gets rolling at any clip it will almost certainly get past the hole. There are other situations that you might determine call for the sit pitch, but the above is the most common.

Walk!

The walk pitch hits the green with a mid-level trajectory and rolls a little bit. You might consider this pitch shot the one you would play most often. When you have enough green between you and the hole that you don't have to be overly concerned with the ball going way past the hole if it runs a little, this is the shot you want to play.

Run!

The run pitch is the shot you want to play when the hole is at the farthest point on the green from you and judging how far to carry the ball the full distance would leave too much room for error and/or misjudgment.

MAKING THE PLAY: THE COMMONS

No matter which of the three types of pitch you decide to play, they each have these things in common:

- **The clubface always aims at the target.** One basic rule that will never fail you in golf: Always aim the clubface at the target. The part of the clubface you aim with is the lead edge. That's the edge at the bottom of the clubface. Don't aim with the top of the club—it's too difficult to get a good fix on the target that way, and not even the world's best players would do it, because the clubface often ends up closed. Whenever you're fixing your aim on a target, the best advice is this: Stand behind the ball and pick out something on the ground in front of your ball that is on the same line your target lies on. Aim the lead edge of the clubface at that spot. Works every time.

- **The butt of the club always points at the center of your body.** This is a pretty easy one to understand. No matter where you position the ball, the grip end of the club should point at the center of your body. This is important to remember, since you'll be changing the position of the ball depending upon whether you wish to play a sit, walk, or run pitch.

- **Always swing along your shoulder line.** What exactly does this mean? To hit each of the various shots, you'll align your shoulders in various positions in relation to the target line. When we say swing along your shoulder line it means that the clubhead should swing along the same line your shoulders are aimed along. For example, if your shoulders are aimed left of the target line, the club should swing along that same line, i.e., it should move away from the ball outside the target line and, after impact, move inside the target line. Here's a key point to remember: Swinging the clubhead along your shoulder line *does not mean you should aim the clubface along your shoulder line.* When we refer to swinging along your shoulder line, we're referring only to the path of movement the club makes once you start to move it. The *aiming of the clubface* and the *path of the clubhead* are two separate things on your checklist of things to do.

- **How far you take the club back and through determines how far the ball will fly.** Each of the three types of pitch shots can be played various distances, and judging the distance is one of the toughest parts of playing any shot in golf. The determining factor in creating distance is how far you take the club back and through the ball. Except for rare situations and unless you're Fred Couples, the length of your backswing and follow-through should be the same. Now, of course, the question is: Is there some sort of formula you can use to determine exactly how far a shot will fly, i.e., if you swing the club back three feet and through three feet, the ball will travel 17.5 yards? The answer is no. The only way you can make this determination is to experiment with it yourself and get a feel for it. Obviously, you can't watch the clubhead go back and forth, so you have to sense how far it has traveled. Try starting out by picking a distance you'd like to play the ball—say, 15 yards—then measure off the yardage and start hitting shots to a target. Pay attention to how "long" the swing feels and you'll start to get the hang of it pretty quickly. There are some other things you'll want to do to get more comfortable with playing shots of a certain distance, but we'll cover them in a bit.

- **The trajectory of the shot is determined by the position of the ball in your stance.** The trajectory of each of these shots is really the key element that separates them. This critical characteristic is determined by where you place the ball in your stance. And while you use your feet to determine the ball's position, the true impact is seen in the ball's relationship to your upper body, specifically the center of your chest. When the ball is to the right of the center of your chest, your arms must reach back toward the ball, and in doing so, you take loft off the club. The more you reach, the more loft you take off the club.

MAKE IT SIT

You've assessed your situation and determined that the pitch shot you wish to play should land softly upon the green and stay in the proximity of where it lands. You want to play the sit pitch. Here's your checklist of things to do:

- You should play this shot with a sand wedge, or even a lob wedge if you want to hit it very high and very short. If you choose the lob wedge, just be sure you know how far you can hit it, and how long of a swing it will require to cover the distance you need.

- Play the ball forward in your stance. This helps you get the maximum effective loft out of the club. Forward in this sense is a relative term—you want to position the ball just a tad to the left of the center of your body. You may see players on TV play dramatic, sky-high flop shots, and it appears that they have the ball played way out in front of them. Don't try to emulate this—keep things in perspective.

- Set up slightly open to your target. This means your feet, knees, hips, and shoulders should be aligned slightly left of the target line. Remember, keep the clubface aimed squarely at the target line.

- If you're attempting to play a longish sit pitch, widen your stance (this gives you more balance for a longer swing) and hold the club at the end of the grip (longer arc, more speed, more distance). If you're attempting to play a shortish sit pitch you'll want to narrow your stance and choke down on the club.

- Swing along your shoulder line and make a conscious effort to complete your follow-through. Swinging along this line will move the clubhead outside the target line moving away from the ball and move it inside the target line just after impact. Something to think about might be this: Keep your right elbow close to your body during this swing.

- Speaking of the follow-through, here's a few things for you to think about. For this shot the knuckles on your left hand should be facing the sky when you have completed the shot. Imagine that there is a mirror on the clubface. You should see yourself in the mirror when you've completed the swing for this shot. These two images will help you keep your left wrist firm through the ball. You can't pull this shot off if the clubhead turns over through the ball.

MAKE IT WALK

- Play the ball in the dead center of your body.
- Align yourself squarely to the target line.
- Swing the club along the target line.
- For a longer shot, widen your stance and hold the club at the end of the grip. For a shorter shot, narrow your stance and choke down on the club.

MAKE IT RUN

- Play the ball back in your stance. Just as when we talk about moving the ball forward, moving the ball *back* is a relative term. It doesn't mean playing the ball back off your right foot. When we say play the ball back we mean move it slightly right of the center of your body—two inches or so should do it. This will place your hands ahead of the club-head, leaning the shaft toward the hole and taking some loft off the club.

- Align your feet, knees, and hips slightly left of your target line, and your shoulders slightly right of your target line. Be careful here to aim only *slightly* right of your target line. If you overdo it, you can smother the ball.

- Swing along the line that points right of your target line. Swinging along this line will move the clubhead inside the target line as it moves away from the ball and take it outside the target line just after impact.

- For a longer shot, widen your stance and hold the club at the end of the grip. For a shorter shot, narrow your stance and choke down on the club.

KNOW WHERE YOU GO

Obviously, the idea with any shot from around the green is to get the ball as close to the hole as possible. The reason for raising this point is that to reach your goal (the hole) you have to realize the distinction between the hole and your target. In all of the shots and situations described above, we use the term *target line*, which of course is a straight line from the ball to your target. Unless you're playing a sit pitch, there's no chance that the hole is your target—and frankly, even if you're playing a sit pitch, you probably shouldn't select the hole as your target, because the ball will roll a little bit.

For any shot you play with the intention of the ball getting airborne, even if it's only for a foot, your target is where you want the ball to *land*, not where you want the ball to come to rest. (On a putt it's different. Your target is the highest point of the break, unless the putt is straight. On a straight putt the hole is your target.) Knowing the difference between your target and the hole is important, because it's the target (and the line that runs from your ball to it) that is the one constant in all the adjustments you must make to play any shot in golf.

So how do you decide what your target is on any given shot? There's a lot of variables that go into deciding where any chip shot or pitch shot should land—and, thus, what your target should be on any given shot. The key factors in determining where you should land your ball are:

- How close you are to the hole.

- How much green surface is between you and the hole.

- The general slope of the ground between you and the hole, and any smaller undulations on the green along the path you see your ball taking as it nears the hole.

- The speed of the green.

There are no general rules that apply to these situations that you can't figure out for yourself using a little common sense. For example, if the green is sloping away from you, the ball is going to roll faster than it would on a flat surface. As a result, you would want to land the ball (your target) farther from the hole than if you were playing to a flat surface. Also, a shot that goes into the green lower will run farther than a shot that goes into the green higher. And so on. Obviously, there are far too many variables to cover every possible situation. The point is that you have to use your best judgment to determine where the ball should land and then determine which of the shots offers the best opportunity to get to that spot with the proper trajectory and velocity so that the ball will end up as close to the hole as possible.

PIT(CH)FALLS

You knew there had to be some. Common mistakes, that is. Here's a few biggies to look out for when you're playing a pitch shot:

- **Opening the clubface, i.e., getting it aimed right of your target.** This is a large one, folks, because it is the precursor of the ugliest shot in golf: the shank. (If you're lucky enough to have never hit a shank, or you don't know what one is, close your eyes and move on to the next paragraph. Spare yourself the torture.) A shank, as you almost certainly and unfortunately are aware, is a shot that travels at a 90 degree angle to the target—in other words, it flies straight right, and that's not a good thing.

   Whither cometh the shank? (What the hell causes it?) The answer is the hosel of the club, the part of the club where the shaft joins the clubhead. When you get the lead edge of the club pointing to the right of your target, the hosel suddenly becomes much more likely to contact the ball. In effect, you're exposing the hosel to the ball. The result: A round ball meant to be contacted by a flat surface is contacted instead by a cylindrical surface that is much smaller than the ball. The ball flight is golf's version of a foul ball.

   So if you ever feel the temptation to "open" the clubface by aiming it right of the target, our advice is simple: Don't.

- **The butt of the grip pointing to the left or the right of the center of your body.** Remember that for each of the pitch shots the butt of the club should be pointing at the center of your body. What happens when you forget this rule? If you get the butt end of the club pointed to the left of the center of your body you've dramatically changed the angle of the club and its effectiveness. The bottoms of your irons (the soles) are shaped so that they will deflect the digging into the ground started by the sharp lead edge as it slips under the ball. As a result, on a properly struck shot the club may make a divot, but it's not detrimental to the shot. When you point the butt of the club left of the center of your body, the deflective quality of the sole (bounce) is eliminated and the lead edge of the club digs straight down into the ground. The ball goes nowhere.

   When you get the end of the club pointed to the right of the center of your body you'll have placed yourself in one of the most uncomfortable positions you could possibly achieve, and you've angled your wrists in the exact opposite positions of where they should be. A bad shot, either fat or bladed (depending upon your timing) will most certainly result. So keep that butt pointed at the center of your gut.

- **Playing the ball too far back or too far forward in your stance.** If you play the ball too far back in your stance, the club will hit the ground before it hits the ball, and that's no good. If you play the ball too far forward in your stance, the club will be on its upward path when it contacts the ball—and it won't make contact on the face. Rather, the lead edge will hit the ball, and that's no good either.

- **Swinging along the target line rather than your body lines.** This isn't an issue if you're playing the walk pitch, since your body lines and your target line are parallel. However, if you're attempting to play the sit pitch (body lines aimed left of the target line) or the run pitch (body lines aimed right of the target line), you have to take care to remember that the clubhead should swing along those body lines. If you swing down the target line when your body is aimed left of the target line, you'll miss your target to the right. You might miss it way right (Mr. Ball, meet Mr. Hosel). If you swing down the target line when your body is aimed right of the target line, you'll miss your target to the left at best. The worst case scenario is that you'll hit it fat.

The Sand Game

Sand. It's the nemesis of nearly every high handicap golfer, and it's the final component of the short game that you need to improve if you're going to break 100. When you get right down to it, there isn't a single good reason that you should fear the sand. Playing a basic sand shot from a fairly good lie in the sand is no more difficult than any of the shots heretofore discussed. The first bit of advice in this area is as follows: Get over it. Don't be afraid of the sand, don't get despondent when your ball goes in the sand. Don't assume you've blown a hole just because you play a shot that ends up in the sand. It's just sand—the same stuff you played in when you were a kid. (And that wasn't so tough, was it?) So let's get down to the business of successfully executing shots from the sand.

BEFORE YOU START TO SCHOOL, MAKE SURE YOU HAVE THE TOOL

Even in this day of advanced equipment technology it's not uncommon to see high handicap golfers attempting to play from the sand using something other than a sand wedge. Since a sand wedge isn't part of the standard set of clubs, some golfers see it as an added and unnecessary expense. After all, a sand wedge doesn't have that much more loft than the pitching wedge (which is included in the standard set). Can't I make do with what I have without spending an extra $100 or so? The answer is, no, you can't make do. To consistently escape from a greenside sand situation, you must have a sand wedge. That's not to say that you have to go out and spend $100 to become a good sand player. Look around in a discount golf shop or check with a local pro to see if you can't find a used sand wedge. There's a good chance you could pick one up for $20, give or take a few bucks.

Here's why you absolutely, positively need a sand wedge if you're serious about breaking 100:

- The sand is softer than the turf surface that makes up the rest of the terra firma part of the golf course. You didn't need this book to tell you that. But what you might not know is that all of the irons in your basic set (your lowest numbered iron through your pitching wedge) are designed to dig into the ground. The flattish sole of the typical iron club is designed to accommodate this digging, and on a properly struck shot, the ground is firm enough to prevent the club from digging too far into it.

- What do you suppose happens once one of these clubs starts digging into the sand? The sand is loose and soft and the club does what anything else would do if it entered sand at a descending angle—it continues to dig down. You're probably familiar with this feeling if you've ever unsuccessfully attempted to play a shot from the sand with a pitching wedge. The club slams into the sand and stays there, and the ball moves an inch or two.

- The sand wedge is designed to prevent this from happening. Rather than having a sole that is flat from front (lead edge) to back, the sand wedge has a curved sole, which gives it a quality known as bounce, because that's exactly what it causes the club to do. Rather than continue digging into the sand once the club has entered it, the sole (and therefore the entire club) deflects off the sand (or bounces off it) and starts traveling up. When the club moves through the sand in this manner it displaces the sand underneath the ball, forcing it and the ball upward. You never actually contact the ball with the club—it rides out of the bunker on a cushion of sand.

If you don't have a sand wedge get one. If you have one, keep reading to find out what you're attempting to do with it and how to do it.

THE GARDEN-VARIETY SAND SHOT

Like any other situation in golf, there are many different scenarios you might encounter in the sand. We'll touch on some of the more difficult ones in sidebars as you move through the following pages, but the main intention here is to help you become proficient at the basic, garden-variety sand shot you would play from a greenside bunker—that is to say, a situation where the ball is sitting cleanly in the sand and you don't have any severe stance considerations. And as with any other shot, you have to pick the place you'd like the ball to land on the green and use it as your target. When you're picking your target, keep in mind that your primary goal any time you're in a bunker is to get out of the bunker. That is to say, you don't necessarily want to settle on a target if it's going to require you to hit a shot you're not comfortable attempting. So select your target based on the fact that your primary concern is getting out of the sand.

As with any other situation, you have to assess the position you're in and where you are in relation to the hole. The closer you are to the hole, the higher and shorter the shot you want to play. The farther you are from the hole, the lower and longer the shot you want to play. No matter how far you are from the hole, you want to play the ball just left of the center of your body.

The height and distance of the shot are influenced by three factors: where you aim the clubface (face), how far into the sand you dig your feet and how open your stance is (your base), and the speed at which you swing the club (the pace). Right there you have the formula for successful sand shots—Face + Base + Pace. Let's break down each of the components individually and then take a look at how they blend together to produce good sand shots.

Face

If your target is close to you, the objective is to play a high, short shot. As the target moves farther away from you, the height of the shot decreases and the distance it should carry in the air increases. The position of the clubface impacts on the height of the shot (other factors impact on the distance, as you'll see in a bit).

The higher you want the ball to fly, the more you want the clubface to be open in relation to your stance. The lower you want the ball to fly, the more square you want the clubface in relation to your stance.

The above warrants some explanation, despite the fact that it is ground we've covered earlier in the book. The clubface *does not open or close in relation to the target.* In other words, you do not aim the clubface either left or right of the target. *You should always aim the lead edge of the clubface at your target.* That's why we say open the clubface in relation to your body. How do you do that? You move your body, not the clubface, until the face is square to the target.

Like any other shot, you should choose your target from behind the ball. Once you select the target do not vary on your point of aim. The lead edge of the clubface should be square to that target. To adjust the height at which the shot will fly adjust your body lines (feet, knees, hips, and shoulders) to the left of your target line. When you make this adjustment, be certain to move all these key body points. Be especially careful not to aim only your shoulders left. The more you aim your body to the left, the higher the shot will fly. That's all you need to know about the "face" part of the equation.

Base

We spent some time at the outset of this discussion on sand talking about how you don't want to dig too far into the sand. However, you do want to dig into the sand to some degree, because it is the sand that moves the ball. One of the difficulties in judging the garden-variety sand shot is this: How much sand do you want to come in contact with?

The biggest influence as to how much sand you hit is the "base" area of the equation. How far you dig your feet into the sand and how far away you stand from the ball are the two components of your base. The first element, how far you dig your feet into the sand, determines how far behind the ball the club will enter the sand. In turn, how far behind the ball the club enters the sand determines how far the ball flies. That's worth repeating: How far from the ball the club enters the sand determines how far the ball will fly. The farther behind the ball the club enters the sand, the shorter it will fly. Ergo, the shorter you want the shot to fly, the farther you dig your feet into the sand.

The relationship doesn't end there (and don't worry, we're going to give you a handy-dandy checklist to sort all of this out). Here's the next part: How far you dig your feet into sand also determines *how much farther away from the ball you stand than you normally would.* For every inch you dig down into the sand with your feet, you should move an inch farther away from the ball than normal.

Let's recap: If you want to play a short shot, you dig your feet farther into the sand and stand farther away from the ball. For a longer shot you would dig your feet in less and stand closer to the ball. For the moment at least, these are the basics you need to grasp for the "base" element.

For a long bunker shot, dig your feet less deep into the sand, and stand closer to the ball.

Shallow swing arc

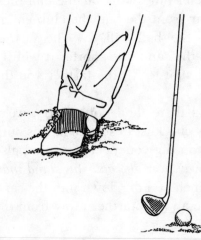

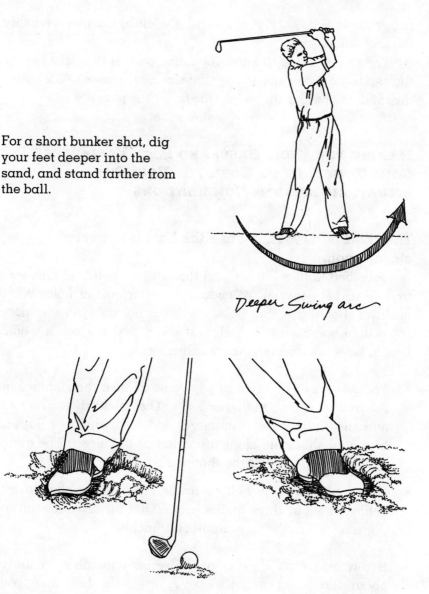

For a short bunker shot, dig your feet deeper into the sand, and stand farther from the ball.

Deeper Swing arc

Pace

The speed at which you swing the club is the "pace" part of the equation. It is comprised of two elements: If you swing the club slowly you'll get a shot that doesn't have much velocity, which has some effect on how much the ball runs once it's on the ground. The quicker you swing the club, the more velocity the shot will have.

The second thing to know regarding pace is this: The harder the sand, the softer the swing (the slower the pace). The softer the sand, the harder the swing (the faster the pace).

MAKING THE FACE, BASE, AND PACE VARIABLES COME TOGETHER TO WORK FOR YOU: THE SITUATIONS AND THE COMBINATIONS

The short bunker shot when the hole is cut very close to you.

Your ball is in a bunker and the hole isn't all that far away from you. Let's say you're about 15 feet from the hole. What qualities should this shot possess? Under normal circumstances you would want it to fly high and short, and not roll a whole bunch. Let's run through the checklist:

- You want it to fly high, so you want to open the clubface in relation to your body quite a bit. That means you want to aim the clubface at your target and aim your feet, knees, hips, and shoulders along a line left of the target. The more left you go, the higher the shot will go.

- You don't want the ball to travel very far, so plan to hit behind it about three inches or so. That means you want to dig your feet in the same number of inches.

- Before you start digging in, however, remember to move about three inches farther away from the ball than you would stand to play a normal pitch shot.

The "medium-size" bunker shot when the hole is cut at a distance that allows you to play a shot that's about half carry and half run.

This is what you might call the standard bunker shot. Whenever you have the chance to run the ball partway to the hole out of the sand you should do so, because the farther the carry, the more difficult the shot is to pull off. To play a shot of "average" height and carry you'll want to do this:

- Aim the clubface at the target and aim your body lines (feet, knees, hips, and shoulders) just slightly left of your target line.

- Plan to hit roughly two inches behind the ball. This means you should dig your feet in two inches and move about two inches farther away from the ball than you would for a normal pitch shot from the same distance.

The long bunker shot, when the hole is cut on the extreme opposite side of the green from you or you're in a bunker that has a few yards between its edge and the beginning of the green.

If you've watched golf on TV at all, you've almost inevitably heard an analyst say something such as "The long bunker shot is the most difficult shot in golf, even for the tour players." True enough, the longer bunker shot isn't the easiest thing you might have to do during a round of golf, but it's not brain surgery either— you can do it. You want the shot to carry longer than a typical shot, so you'll want to hit it a little bit lower. Try this technique:

- Use a pitching wedge instead of a sand wedge.

- Aim the clubface directly at the target.

- Aim your body lines parallel to your target line.

- Plan to hit about one inch behind the ball.

- Dig in one inch with your feet, and stand an inch or so farther away from the ball than you would for a pitch shot of the same length.

SOME FINAL TOUCHES FOR YOUR SAND GAME

For someone struggling to break 100, playing shots from the sand seems complex and demanding. The high handicapper visualizes the sand shot and thinks that it requires a great amount of timing, judgment, and precision. The truth is that playing shots from the sand requires less precision than any other phase of the game. That's right, friend—greenside bunker shots allow more room for error than any shot in the game.

The most common point of confusion among high handicappers is that they don't know how much sand they should take. Using the basic schemes described above, you won't have to worry about that. *But just to be safe, here's the two main concerns in this area: How far behind the ball should I hit, and how deep into the sand should the club go?* The answer to the first part is laid out for you above. Regarding how deep into the sand the club should go, you don't have to worry about that if you make sure you move away from the ball the corresponding number of inches. This will force you to swing the club at the proper angle. So as long as you remember your rules, you don't have to worry about those two things.

Here's another common problem: *Sometimes I hit it too heavy, and sometimes I don't hit any sand at all and the ball goes flying across the green. What's up with that?* That's how the cycle usually goes: You blade one across the green and the next time you're in the sand you hit so far behind the ball it doesn't budge. Here's the story: The reason we say there's more room for error with sand shots than there is for any other shot is because, in essence, *you're trying to hit the shot fat.* Think about it. You're trying to hit behind the ball when you play a sand shot, so hitting it thin should never be an issue. Here's a *guaranteed* way to avoid hitting the ball thin from the sand. *Don't choke down on the club—hold it at the very end of the grip. When you lower yourself into the sand you're guaranteeing you'll hit it fat.* By using the rules above regarding how far to hit behind the ball, how far to dig in, and how far to stand from the ball, you'll make sure you get the proper amount of sand.

PUBLIC ENEMY NUMBER ONE

The most common mistake high handicap golfers make in the sand is this: They stick the club into the sand and leave it there, because they are afraid to hit the ball too far. So here's the tip: *You absolutely, positively have to follow through on every single shot you play from the sand.* (Okay, there is one exception, but we'll cover that in a moment.) *It is imperative that you keep the clubhead moving through the ball and down your shoulder line.* That's all there is to say about it. If you slow down the clubhead as you swing through the ball, it's a guaranteed death move. *You must accelerate the clubhead through the ball. Hopefully, the excessive use of italic type in this paragraph has made it clear to you that it is vital to swing through the ball.*

Why is this so important? If you remember back to the introduction of sand shots, we described how the ball flies out of the bunker on the sand you displace as the club travels through the sand. *If you don't follow through—if you don't accelerate the clubhead through the ball—you won't displace any sand, and the ball won't go anywhere. Nowhere. Nada. Zilch.* So, swing through the ball. It's that simple.

HOW TO HANDLE A BURIED LIE

The toughest situation from the sand for the high handicap golfer is when the ball is buried in the sand. In this situation the garden-variety sand shot technique isn't going to get the job done for you. When the ball is buried down in the sand you can't get the club deep enough into the sand to successfully dislodge the ball. This type of buried lie (sometimes referred to as a "fried egg" because, well, that's what it looks like) requires a technique that is entirely different and almost completely opposite of the garden-variety sand shot.

Here's the technique:

1. First, all you're trying to do is get the ball out of the sand. Don't have any expectations for the shot beyond that.

2. Move the ball back in your stance. Way back. Play it well right of the center of your body. Split the difference between the center of your body and your right foot.

3. Close your body in relation to the target, i.e., aim your body lines right of the target.

4. Close the face of the club in relation to the spot you're aiming at—aim the lead edge to the left of that spot.

5. Swing as hard as you can without losing your balance, and slam the clubhead into the sand about an inch behind the ball. Don't try to follow through. Just leave the club in the sand.

6. The ball will pop out onto the green and run quite a bit.

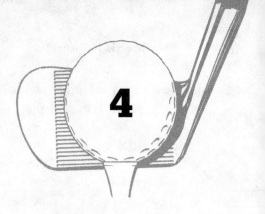

Course
Management
for Dummies

(AND A FEW TIPS ON THE SUBJECT FOR SMART PEOPLE LIKE YOU)

Who knows how 100 got to be the Holy Grail for the high handicap player? Things evolve for funny reasons and in funny ways when it comes to golf. Take, for example, the idea of a bogey being a bad thing. Originally, a bogey was a good thing. You read that right—a bogey was a good thing. During the early days of golf, a player would play a match against an imaginary competitor—Colonel Bogey. Colonel Bogey played each hole in the number of strokes that a good (not expert) golfer would require to play the hole. As a result, when a golfer played a round in bogey, he had played a fine round. A problem arose, however. When the very good or expert player made a score better than bogey, he needed to refer to it as something. That's how the term "par" came into use.

But guess what? Another problem arose out of the usage of the term "par." Because by nature people insist on comparing themselves to the very best as opposed to the typical (or average), golfers started to compare their scores to par instead of bogey. It's not hard to comprehend, really. The idea of being "average" does not at all appeal to people. Everyone wants to think that they are better than average. As a result, a word (bogey) that was intended to symbolize a well-played hole came to mean that which was worse than average. And a word that was meant to symbolize superb play (par) came to be synonymous with "average." In fact, "par" was equated with averageness to such an extent that it became part of the everyday lexicon in English-speaking countries. In reality, however, par was the ultimate, not the average.

Right about now you might be wondering just what in the world this has to do with your breaking 100. The fact is, it has plenty to do with your reaching your goal. The reason for the above is to help you place in context the idea that is about to follow. And that idea is this: To facilitate your progress toward breaking 100, you have to set goals that are not only reachable but conducive to satisfying your ego. To do that you've got to do something that might seem simple but is, in fact, pretty drastic for the average person: You have to stop comparing your performance to the people with whom you play, and you must stop comparing your scores to what is considered "standard" within the game. (Remember, what is now routinely considered "standard" [par] is actually expert play.) As your game improves you can start to compare your performance to the "standards." In the meantime you have to set up a realistic system of measuring your progress—a personal system—in your march toward shattering 100. The system of Personal Par as described below is the first of four cornerstones in managing your game so that you can consistently break 100. The other three are knowing how far on average you hit each club in your bag; developing a strength and weakness profile (which is much easier than it sounds); the recognition of various situations and scenarios and how they dictate the shot you should play.

Breaking 100: This Time It's Personal

Right this second, as you read this, you're being introduced to a new way of assessing your performance. It's called Personal Par, and here's how it works:

- **If a hole measures 180 yards or less, you should consider it a par three.** This is nothing new to you—every hole of this distance is a par three on the scorecard, too.

- **If a hole measures between 180 and 380 yards, you should consider it a par four.** On the high end of the scale, i.e., more toward the 380 yard end, this shouldn't seem all that odd to you. A 380-yard hole, after all, is normally a par four, as is just about any hole that measures more than 240 yards. What may seem a bit out of sorts for you is the idea that you should treat a 180-yard hole as a par four. Seem a bit ludicrous? Hang in there, pal, and read on.

- **If a hole measures between 380 and 500 yards, you should consider it a par five.** Once again, on the high end of the scale this doesn't seem to be out of line. On the low end, however, a 380-yard par five? Yes, a 380-yard par five. You'll get used to it. Keep reading.

- **Any hole that measures more than 500 yards is, in your book, a par six.** Now you're thinking, "Whooooooa. Just a minute here. There's no such thing as a par six! You boys are talking crazy talk now." You *do* want to break 100, don't you? So lighten up. The idea of a par six isn't all that crazy—besides, there are actual par sixes out there in the world. Not a whole bunch of them, but they exist.

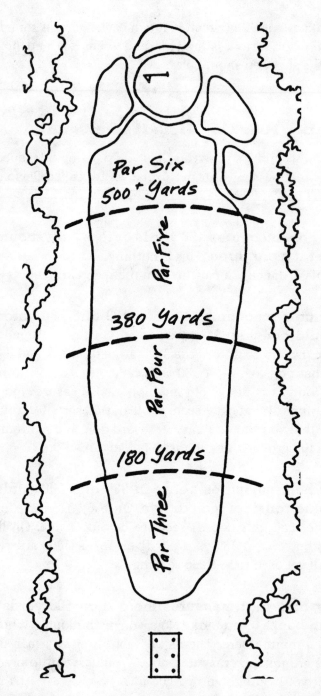

In the Personal Par system, holes under 180 yards are played as par threes; between 180 and 380 is a par four; 380 to 500 is a par five; anything over 500 is a par six.

Personal Par for Women

If you're a woman and you're on a mission to break 100, here's an adjusted scale for your Personal Par. It's not meant to assume that you lack the ability to hit the ball as far as a man. It's simply scaled down to match the distances of holes that an average woman golfer plays when she plays from the tees designated for women. So here's your Personal Par scheme:

- If the hole measures 120 yards or less, you should play it as a par three under your Personal Par system.

- If the hole measures 120 yards to 300 yards, you should consider it a par four.

- If the hole measures between 300 and 420 yards, you should consider it a par five.

- If the hole measures more than 420 yards, play it as a par six.

Your Personal Par System: Understand It, Learn to Love It, Use It to Your Advantage

The Personal Par System might seem a bit dramatic to you on the surface. After all, the idea that you might treat a 181-yard hole as a par four (or a 121-yard hole as a par four if you're a woman) probably seems absolutely preposterous to you. In order for the Personal Par System to work for you, you need to consider it in the proper light. To do so, you must grasp the understanding of what it means to play a hole in "regulation par." To understand the term "regulation" in golf you have to count backwards, starting with the number that represents the traditional par on a given hole. Once you know what the par is, subtract two from it. The two represents the number of putts an expert player is likely to take on any green, no matter the par for the hole. Whatever you have left after you subtract the two from the par is the number of shots it would typically take an expert player to reach the green. As a result, on a par three the expert player is expected to reach the green in one shot, on a par four in two shots, and on a par five in three shots, regardless of the length of the hole. If a player's ball is on the green after the prescribed number of shots for a given hole, that person is said to have *hit the green in regulation*. (This is a useful phrase, and we're going to get back to it in a moment.) If that same person then takes two putts to hole out, they have played the hole in *regulation par*.

The usage of the word *regulation* itself doesn't entirely make sense, but just as *par* has come to mean something other than what it was intended to mean, so too has *regulation* entered the golf lexicon to an extent that it's easier to adapt it to your needs than to come up with an altogether new word.

In case you've never thought about it, the entire idea of *par* and *regulation* evolved out of the idea that a certain sequence of events would *typically* occur. That is to say that a person just might hit the green in regulation and need only one putt to hole out, but that is the exception rather than the expected. Likewise, a player can (and very often does) make a par after missing the green in the regulation number of shots (i.e., the second shot on a par four is not on the green), but it's more likely that the person will not par the hole.

The idea behind the Personal Par System is to provide you with a realistic method of comparing your current ability to the hole you're about to play, and of setting your own standards for what will typically happen under certain circumstances. Once you embrace the Personal Par System and start to assess holes differently, you'll start to realize that not quite so much is expected of you, and that you can easily break 100 by modifying your goals and the strategy you use to reach those goals. Stringing together 18 goals that you know you can achieve and then achieving them is much easier than striving for 18 goals set for the expert player. The 18 goals of which we speak are, of course, the 18 holes on a golf course.

Putting Personal Par to Work

Now that you've modified the standard goal of par to your Personal Par it's time to take a look at the strategies that will help you achieve your Personal Par. The idea of *hitting the green in regulation* is still a good measuring stick for your tee-to-green game, so you'll want to begin the process of assessing a given hole by determining how many shots you have to reach the green from the tee. You can and should completely disregard the par for the hole as listed on the scorecard. When you arrive at the tee for a hole, check the distance of the hole to determine your Personal Par. Having done that, use the minus two formula to figure out how many shots you can use to reach the green. That should work out like this:

- If the hole is 180 yards or less, your Personal Par is three, and you should be able to hit the green in a single shot.

- If the hole is between 181 yards and 380 yards, your Personal Par is four, and you should be able to hit the green with two well-played shots.

- If the hole is between 381 yards and 500 yards, your Personal Par is five, and you should be able to hit the green with three well-played shots.

- If the hole is more than 500 yards long, your Personal Par is six, and you should be able to hit the green with four well-played shots.

  For women, the shot displacement works out as follows:

- If the hole is 120 yards or less, your Personal Par is three, and you should be able to hit the green with one well-played shot.

- If the hole is between 121 yards and 300 yards, your Personal Par is four, and you should be able to reach the green with two well-played shots.

- If the hole is between 301 and 420 yards, your Personal Par is five, and you should be able to reach the green with three well-played shots.

- If the hole is more than 420 yards, your Personal Par is six, and you should be able to reach the green with four well-played shots.

It's important for you to know how many shots you *can* use to reach each green before you start play on each hole. Why is that? You should consider the number of shots you can use as a resource. To use an everyday analogy, let's say you can look at these shots as dollars in a bank. Before you use one of the dollars, you want to have a clear idea of what you're going to gain as a result of spending it. Likewise with your shot resources on each hole you play. You should know exactly what you're going to get out of a shot before you expend it so that the *total investment in shots on the hole pays the biggest return*. If you have two shots to reach a certain green, consider the two shots investments of equal weight and value that will pay off in your ball being on the green. To do this, you have to play two shots that are mutually beneficial for each other. In other words, attempting to play the longest possible shot you can from the tee is usually not necessary, and it isn't always that wise, either. Why? Because the longer shots mean less loft on the club, and less loft on the club means it's more likely the shot will drift off line. When shots drift off line they get into trouble—trees, bunkers, water, out-of-bounds, illegal crossing of state lines, etc. Also, a longer shot requires a longer swing, which creates more room for error in the swinging action, which creates a higher probability of bad stuff happening.

Becoming a World Class Manager

At its roots, the Personal Par System is an attempt to remove the blinders and allow you to see that the number of options you have on any given hole are much more numerous than is obvious at first glance. When a golf course is designed, the architect has a definite idea in mind for the way the hole should be played, and in effect, the design of the hole is an attempt to lead you by the nose through the hardest part of the challenge. Tees are aimed in the direction the architect wishes you to take. Haz-

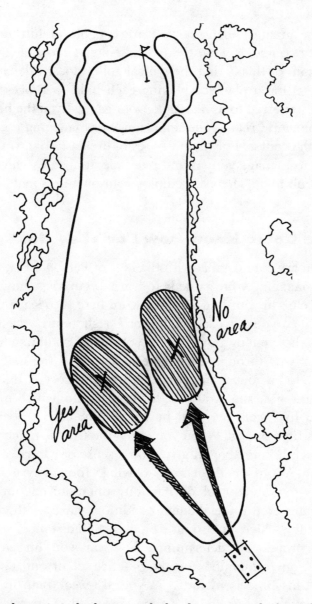

The bad player is in lockstep with the designer right from the tee—hit the driver, aim at the flag. You have to learn how to play from dot to dot.

ards and whatnot are placed in the area toward which the archi-tect would like you to drive the ball, and it is expected that you will play the club which, if perfectly struck, will make the ball travel the greatest distance you are capable of hitting a ball. Which, of course, is what the typical golfer almost always does. The reason for this is that the typical golfer doesn't devote much time to setting a plan for playing each hole—a process that is otherwise referred to as *managing your game*. Even the best players in the world realize the importance of managing their game around the course. For the purposes of breaking 100, you'll want to learn to manage your round one hole at a time, which is not too difficult to do when you employ your own Personal Par.

You've Got to Know How Far They Go

Once you are comfortable with the idea of Personal Par, the next step in managing your game is to learn, *on average*, how far you hit each club in your bag. The key word here is to learn the *average* distance you hit each club. Perfect shots are nice, but we don't hit them enough to make use of them in building a plan to plot your way through each hole and around the golf course. You have to be honest and current with this process. It shouldn't include the best shot you ever hit in your life, which may have occurred five years ago and has, naturally, become better and better as time passes. When you know the true distance you can hit each club in the bag, it gives you a sense of control and logic when you're out on the course playing. Too many golfers are mentally out of control or mentally unorganized out on the course, and even under benign conditions have a difficult time determining which club to hit from a certain distance.

The process of determining how far you hit each club requires some time alone on the practice tee or out on the golf course. This time is included in your 13-week plan in the last chapter of this book, but it's time you need to invest right up front before you begin doing just about any of the other things in this book that are related to the long game. To get the time alone on the practice tee or the golf course, you're going to have to do one of two things—get there real early or stay real late. Our suggestion is to try to accomplish this on the practice tee and to try it late in the day on a day that the wind is calm. Most golfers only use the practice tee to warm up before a round, and there's not much of that going on later in the day after the last groups have teed off. (We realize, of course, that you can only do what's realistic for you—so do the best you can.) Also, it's not real common to go wandering around in the middle of a practice range, and you'll need to be hitting to an area that isn't littered with a million other range balls. To be able to do this, you'll have to enlist the aid of the person who manages the range. Explain to them what you are doing ("I'm following a 13-week plan to break 100, and I need to figure out how far I hit each of my clubs. . . ") and ask them when would be the best time to do it. The two things you should tell them you need: A range empty (or close to it) of people and of scattered balls on the ground.

Once you've figured out a place and the best time to do this, you can knock it out in a handful of practice sessions. In fact, it's probably not a good idea to try to figure it out all at once. You would end up hitting way too many balls than would be useful for you. (We know you hear stories of tour players who beat balls on the range until their hands bleed, but they're conditioned to it, and beyond that, they've got nothing better to do.) Follow this routine:

- It's hard to say how many practice balls you'll get in a bag or a bucket, but dump them out and divide them into piles that consist of 12 balls each. If you have any extras just divide them up among the piles.

- This isn't like getting fit for a suit, so keep in mind that there isn't anything terribly precise about it. You're just trying to get an idea for the average distance you hit each club.

- Start with the clubs that will give you a representative sampling of how far you can hit a group of clubs in general. In other words, the first time you do it, decide you're going to use your 9-iron, 5-iron, and 7-wood. You can fill in the gaps in subsequent practice sessions.

- Select a target for your 9-iron shots and hit shots toward it. You should always have a target whenever you're working on distance and direction. (When you're working on swing mechanics, the target goes out the window, but that's a different story.)

- After you hit a shot, make a mental note as to whether it was a one (perfect), a two (average), or a three (yikes!). Continue to hit the rest of the pile and make these mental notes.

- Once you've hit the 12 balls with the 9-iron, pace off the distance from where you are to the core group of balls. Chances are, these will consist mostly, but not entirely, of the balls you designated "two." When we say core group we're talking strictly about distance; it doesn't mean they have to be clustered near your target. Don't count the three balls that went farthest, and don't count the three shortest ones either. (This goes a lot faster if you can enlist the aid of a friend in marking where the balls land.)

- Continue on hitting the groups of 12 with your 5-iron and then your 7-wood. Again, don't count the three longest or the three shortest. Pace them off and come up with an average distance for the clubs.

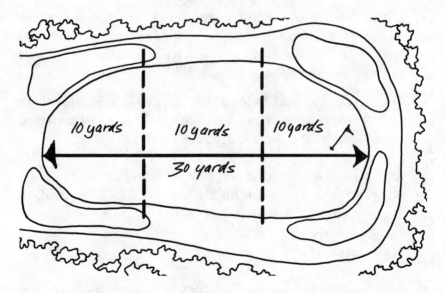

When choosing a club for an approach shot, remember that most greens are three clubs deep (30 yards). So create a mental image of a green divided into three sections for added accuracy.

Over the course of a few weeks, work your way through the set. Give each of your clubs three of these 12-ball mini distance tests and keep track of the results. After three run-throughs with each club you'll have a real good idea of how far you hit each club on average.

One of the things to keep in mind as you run through this process is to not get bogged down in mechanics. It helps enormously if you keep this process as simple as possible. Just pick the target and fire away.

The idea behind noting whether you consider the shot as a "one," a "two," or a "three" is helpful to you in establishing a feel for how shots should feel, and will also help you sort the shots out once you get out to the balls after pacing them off. As the level of your game progresses you can start to strive for more "ones."

One other very important thing to keep in mind is this: This series of 12-ball mini tests for distance should be done on days when the conditions are fairly benign. If it's excessively windy or cold or rainy, don't do it. (If you even think about practicing when it's snowing you really should reexamine your priorities in life.) The most common deterrent is wind. You can be the judge about how windy is too windy, but if you're watching the news and the clown pointing at the magnetic clouds says, "You can expect wind of up to 10 miles per hour or more tomorrow," you can write off your practice session, at least in the sense of accurately determining how far you can hit the ball with each club.

EVEN WHEN YOU KNOW HOW FAR THEY GO, THEY DON'T ALWAYS GO THAT FAR

Common sense would tell you that there must be factors that affect the ball while it's in flight, and therefore either make the ball fly farther or shorter or higher or lower. And your common sense is correct—there's a difference between measured yardage and actual effective yardage. *You want to base your club selection on effective yardage, not on measured yardage.* Here's a list of things that can impact on how far your ball travels once it gets airborne:

- This probably won't come as a news flash to you, but when you're hitting into the wind, the ball won't fly as far.

- When you're hitting with the wind at your back, the ball will fly farther and won't have enough backspin on it to stop once it hits the green. So if the design of the hole allows for it, plan to bounce your ball onto the green. In other words, hit one club less than you normally would under normal conditions.

- With a left-to-right wind, any shot that is curving left-to-right on its own will fly farther, and the curve will be increased. The same goes for right-to-left winds and right-to-left shots. In combination, they increase the distance the ball carries and the amount it curves.

- With a left-to-right wind, a shot that curves into the wind (right-to-left) will fly shorter and curve less—possibly even flying essentially straight. The same is true when the wind is coming from the right—any shot curving into it will fly shorter and straighter than if there were no wind.

- A shot played from an uphill lie (when your body is angled away from the target) will fly higher and shorter. How much higher and how much shorter depends on the severity of the slope. The steeper the slope, the higher and shorter the shot.

- A shot played from a downhill lie (when your body is angled toward the target) will fly lower and longer. Again, how much lower and how much longer depends on the severity of the slope. The steeper the slope, the lower and longer the ball will fly.

- If you're in the rough and the grass is leaning in the direction that you want to play the shot, the ball will fly somewhat farther if you catch it clean. If you don't catch it clean, it won't matter.

- If you're in the rough and the grass is leaning toward you, in the opposite direction that you intend on playing the shot, the ball will not fly as far—no way, no how, not even if you catch it clean.

With the grass leaning toward the hole, the ball will travel farther.

With the grass leaning away from the hole, the ball will fly a shorter distance.

- If you're playing in cold weather, the ball will not fly as far as it normally would.

- If you're playing in hot weather and it's not humid (someplace like the desert), the ball will fly farther than it normally would.

- If it's humid—humid like you can feel the air hanging on your body—the ball will not fly as far. Doesn't matter how hot it is.

- If you're playing at an extremely high altitude, where the air is thin, the ball will fly much farther than typical.

- If you're playing to an elevated green or a green that is below you, 30 feet of elevation change equals 10 yards of true distance change. So if the green is 30 feet above the fairway, you would tack 10 yards onto the measured distance. If the green is 30 feet below the fairway, you would subtract 10 yards from the measured distance. (One yard of elevation equals one yard of distance.)

- If you're playing in the morning and there is dew on the fairways, the ball will fly farther from the short cut grass. Typically it will fly shorter from the longer wet grass in the rough.

- The air over water is more dense than it is over dry land. So if you're attempting a carry over a lake or a pond and the farthest point of the carry is toward the end of the shot, you might want to consider hitting an extra club. If the carry is right in front of you when the ball is traveling at maximum velocity, don't sweat it.

Building Your Strength and Weakness Profile

So far we've covered two of the cornerstone areas that you need to understand to effectively manage your game, namely the concept of Personal Par and the idea that you need to know how far you hit each club. Now it's time to move on to the third cornerstone idea, that of developing a strength and weakness profile. If this sounds boring and complicated, it's not. In fact, you probably already have a pretty good idea of what constitutes your strengths and weaknesses. This process will simply give you a way to quantify your strengths and weaknesses, so you can separate them in a manner that will fit them into the overall plan for improving your level of game management.

If you asked successful people in almost any sport or business pursuit what makes them successful, there would be a commonality in the answers: Know your strengths and exploit them to the fullest. It's highly likely that you, as a high handicap golfer, have fewer strengths than weaknesses, but that's common, and there's nothing wrong with that. Even if you can identify only one strength upon which you can rely, that is enough to start to improve your scoring. (And, eventually, you would start to practice and improve upon the next strength until you felt all areas of your game were modestly proficient. Then you would reverse the process and start to concentrate heavily on improving your weaknesses. But we're getting ahead of ourselves here.) There's nothing at all wrong with going to your strengths over and over and over again. All champions and championship teams do it. So should you.

Figuring Out Your "Go To" Clubs

Every professional golfer has a "go to" shot. In the final round of the 1988 U.S. Open, Curtis Strange didn't feel particularly confident in his driver, so he decided that any time he needed to use it he would play a shot that he knew would end up in the fairway—a modified cut/block shot with the driver that didn't go especially far. The point is that he had complete confidence in his ability to control its direction. In the heyday of the San Francisco 49ers, Jerry Rice was Joe Montana's "go to" guy—the player he looked to in the clutch. The analogies can go on and on. The point is, identifying your strengths is a matter of knowing which shots you can "go to" with confidence. In your case, they won't be as complicated as Curtis Strange's situation described above. In fact, what you're really trying to identify is your "go to" *clubs*—the club(s) in which you have faith.

Here's the amazingly simple process you should follow to decide your "go to" clubs:

- A typical trip to the practice range for the high handicap golfer is a helter skelter affair, with clubs being selected at random and the driver being pounded on for 98 percent of the time. For the purposes of determining your strength and weakness profile, we're going to change that. (And we'll change it for good later on in this book.)

- Instead of just blasting the balls, break them up into clusters and divide the shots into short shots (100 yards or less, and be sure to include short chips and pitches) that you play with your wedges and 9-iron, medium-length shots that you play with your 8-iron, 7-iron, and 6-iron, and longer shots that you play with your 5-iron, 4-iron (if you carry one), your fairway woods, especially your 7-wood, and tee shots you play with your driver and other fairway woods (including the 7-wood again). Obviously, this final group should be played teed up.

- Pick a target for each club within a given group and play toward it as if you were playing an actual shot on the course. For each ball you hit, go through the routine of picking a target and getting your body aimed properly toward it. Then fire away. Just as when you were hitting the "distance" shots above, don't get caught up in mechanics.

- As you hit each shot, again use the designations of "one" (damn, that was good), "two" (wasn't bad), or "three" (butt ugly). You should rate the shots based on how good they felt, how close to the distance you expected them to fly they actually did fly, and how close (or at least how much on line) they were to the target. So if you hit a shot that feels great, ends up near your target, and covers about the distance you expected it to, give it a one. (And by the way, it doesn't necessarily have to fly straight. Judge the accuracy based on where it ends up, not what it looks like in flight.)

- This is pretty simple so far, isn't it? Now all you have to do is determine which group of shots (the short ones, the medium ones, the long ones, or the tee shots) had the most "ones" in it. Then slot the other three groups in descending order.

- As you might have guessed by now, *what you want to identify is not individual "go to" clubs, but a "go to" group of clubs.* So you want to categorize the four groups in descending order from strongest to weakest.

- Once you determine the order of your "go to" groups, you should figure out which clubs within each group you feel most comfortable using. This will come into play, particularly from the tee, at the same time as your "go to" groups do, but the "go to" groups are the key element in determining how you play each hole based on Personal Par.

- Follow this "go to" grouping method of practice for five practice sessions, so you can feel comfortable with the decisions you make on your strengths and weaknesses.

- One final note: Don't combine this process with the distance process. You should keep them separate. Practice is much more efficient when you isolate goals rather than trying to combine them.

Now you understand three of the four cornerstones: the concept of Personal Par; how far you can hit each club; and which group of shot types is your strongest, next strongest, and so on. It's time to move on to the final cornerstone—assessing on-course situations and understanding how to apply your strengths to make the best of those situations.

THE ANALYST: ASSESSING YOUR STRENGTHS AND WEAKNESSES BY THE NUMBERS

Some people, and perhaps you're one of them, might not enjoy spending a whole bunch of time on the practice range. Or perhaps you might like a much more methodical manner of putting together your strength and weakness profile. Maybe you would rather just play instead of practice. The good news for you is that you can put together a strength and weakness profile while you're playing a round—or if you have a great memory you can do it after the round. By keeping a fairly detailed account of your shots, you can develop a strength and weakness profile by keeping track of the following items in your round. You can either keep track in a little notebook or sit down after your round and mentally replay it, making notes as you do:

- How many fairways did you "hit" from the tee? That means, how often did your ball end up in the fairway on driving holes (holes other than par threes)?

- How many greens did you hit in regulation (how many times did your ball end up on the green in two shots less than par for the hole)?

- How many times did you get "up and down" during your round? That means when you missed the green with a shot that would have put you on the green in regulation, how many times did you still make par (with a chip or pitch and a single putt)?

By keeping track of these numbers you can put together a statistically based strength and weakness profile. The basic idea in breaking down the numbers is this: If you hit more fairways than greens, your driving is stronger than your medium-length shots. If you miss more fairways than greens, your driving is a definite weakness, and so on.

The Fourth Cornerstone: Red Lights, Yellow Lights, and Green Lights

By now you should have a good idea of your strengths and weaknesses, and now we're going to talk about how you put them to use on the course. Everyone reading this book is familiar with the symbolism of red lights, yellow lights, and green lights—at least we certainly hope so. (If not, please alert us before you take your next drive anywhere in the United States.) Just in case, however, here's a quick refresher course: *A red light means* STOP! *A yellow light means* CAUTION—WHAT YOU'RE ABOUT TO DO COULD BE VERY COSTLY! *A green light means* GO FOR IT! NOT EVEN YOU CAN SCREW THIS UP! PROBABLY NOT, ANYWAY.

Hopefully, that refresher course wasn't too grueling, but you might be wondering just what the hell it has to do with your golf game. And here's the answer: You're going to learn to break down every shot *before you hit it* and assign it one of the three color designations. So before you even choose the club you're going to play the shot with, you have to decide whether you're in a red light, yellow light, or green light situation.

There are simple rules you can use to decide if a situation is a red light, yellow light, or green light registration. These rules involve only rudimentary math, such as the ability to add the numbers zero, one, two, and three. We're confident you can handle that (heck, if we can, anyone can). What you're going to learn to do is assess the "conditions" of each shot and make your color designation based on those conditions. A condition can be any of several things, and they will be laid out for you in just a moment. Before you start to read the conditions, however, keep these simple rules in mind: If there are no conditions, you're in a green light situation. If there is one condition, you're in a yellow light situation. If there are two or more conditions, you're in a red light situation.

Driving Conditions

- If there are a significant number of trees on one side of the driving area, that is a single condition. If there are trees on both sides of the driving area, that's two conditions.

- If the wind is blowing significantly in any direction, but especially a crosswind or a headwind, that's a condition.

- If there is water on one side of the hole or directly in front of you in the driving area, that's a single condition. If there's water on two sides, that's two conditions (and the course architect should be tarred and feathered).

- If there is sand on one side of the driving area, that's a single condition. Sand on both sides of the driving area equals two conditions.

- If there is any sort of steep drop-off on either side of the driving area—steep enough that your ball might be irretrievable or lost if it travels down that gorge—that's a condition.

- Out of bounds on one side of the driving area is a condition. Out of bounds on both sides of the driving area is two conditions (and a reason to hang the architect after you've tarred and feathered him).

- Any severely deep rough—deep enough that you can spot it from the tee or you know it from prior experience—is a condition. Deep, deep rough on both sides is two conditions.

- If you're playing in the desert, any desert areas are a condition. And it's not at all unusual to have desert on both sides of a landing area, and thus two conditions.

- If your predominant shot pattern is right-to-left or left-to-right, that's a condition.

After you've played your drive, you have to give your next shot a color designation. The conditions are now a bit different:

- First you have to check the lie. If the ball is sitting down in the grass, i.e., if the grass is as high as the top of the ball, that's a condition.

- If the grass is leaning away from your target—leaning against you—that's a condition.

- If your ball is in a divot, that's a condition.

- If your ball is in the sand in a fairway bunker, that's a condition.

- Similar to above, if a significant wind is blowing across or in your face, that's a condition.

- If there is water in front of you or on either side of your target, that's a condition.

- If there is a bunker on one side of your target, that's a condition. If there's a bunker on both sides of your target, that's two conditions.

- When you're playing approaches to the green, the hole position also figures into things. If the hole is cut on the right side of the green and there is a bunker on the right side of the green, that's two conditions. Same goes for when the hole is cut on the left side of the green and there is a bunker on the left side of the green.

- And, once again, if you have a predominant ball flight, that's a condition. If you hit the ball left-to-right on almost every swing, that's a condition. Same goes if you hit the ball consistently from right-to-left.

Now for the Bad News: You Need to Do the Math. Now for the Good News: Anyone Can Do This Math

In the above listings, the conditions are offered up for the most part as single conditions. In some instances, just for clarity and/or to serve as an example, we've combined two conditions. What you have to do in a given situation is to look at all of the possible conditions and add them up. So, if you're facing a shot that is sitting on a perfect lie (no condition), a strong wind is coming from the left (one condition), the hole is cut on the right side of the green (one condition), and there is a bunker on the right side of the green (yet another condition), you're dealing with three conditions and that's a big red light. In this case, the red light is telling you not to aim at the flag. Simply play a shot that will get the ball somewhere on the middle of the green. The above is a sample of the process you would use on playing any shot of 100 yards or more into a green. On shots into the green, the red light, yellow light, green light scenario refers to whether you will aim at the hole. In a red light situation, you should play for the center of the green. In a yellow light situation, it's advisable for you to do so, but hey, we can't make up your mind for you. If you want to shoot at the flag with one condition, have at it. Just realize there's a bit of risk involved. In a green light situation, you can fire right at the flagstick.

The rule hidden above is worth restating: *On any full shot (100 yards or more) where your objective is to place the ball on the green, the red light, yellow light, green light system applies to whether you should attempt to play directly at the hole. Red light, play for the center of the green. Yellow light, you should* probably *aim for the center of the green. Green light, aim at the hole.*

Seeing in Color Begins at the Tee

Since you need to apply these designations to every shot you play, the process obviously starts on the tee of each hole. To accurately assess the tee shot, you will put the other three cornerstones of effective course management to use. Let's use a sample scenario to explain the process of how the four elements all come together:

The first hole of the course you're playing is a 391-yard hole. On the scorecard it is listed as a par four. You, however, will assign yourself a Personal Par of five for this hole. This changes things dramatically for you. Since the hole is now a par five, your goal is to get the ball onto the green in three shots, take two putts, and make your Personal Par.

The next step is to assess the opening shot on the hole and assign it a color designation. Let's say that you've determined through trial and error that you are a very poor driver of the golf ball—and by driver we mean shots played specifically with the driver. Since that's the case, you would almost never hit your driver, because *when you begin to assess the situation from the tee, the red light, yellow light, green light scheme should be used with the idea of placing the drive in the fairway at a distance that will allow you to execute the second shot (or third shot) so that you can hit the green in Personal Par regulation.*

So, going back to the example we've started: The landing area for the tee shot has a bunker on the left side (one condition) and the wind is blowing toward that bunker (a second condition). This is clearly a red light scenario for your driver. But that doesn't matter, because your goal on this hole is to keep the ball in the fairway and hit it a distance that will allow you to reach the green with two more solid, comfortable shots. Let's suppose that in creating your strength and weakness profile you determined that you are just hell-on-wheels with your 7-wood—you nearly always hit it straight and you hit it about 170 yards, give or take a few yards. Now you do some quick math: If you hit the

7-wood and it carries 170 yards and you're in the fairway, you'll have roughly how far left to the green? About 220 yards—a distance you can cover with two 9-iron shots. Since you're trying to hit the green in three shots, playing the 7-wood from the tee suddenly seems like a very viable option, doesn't it?

From the tee your absolute priority is getting the ball in the fairway, because once you miss the fairway, many things can happen and all of them are bad. If this means you can hit as little as a 5-iron off the tee to ensure hitting the fairway, do it. How do you know if you can hit a 5-iron? Do the math for the hole. You know how far you hit your 5-iron, you know how far that will leave you from the green, and you know how many shots you have at your disposal to hit the green in Personal Par regulation.

This type of evaluation from the tee is critical, because we know from experience that the biggest problem high handicappers have from the tee is placing the ball in the fairway. Why is this the case? Because the typical golfer falls into lockstep with the course architect—off the tee, hit driver, then aim at the flag. How many times do you see a high handicapper, including yourself, simply step up to the tee with the goal of keeping the ball in play. Hardly ever, probably never. It helps to look at the game from this viewpoint: It's merely a big game of connect the dots. The first dot is determined by the red light, yellow light, green light system, combined with the knowledge of how far you hit certain clubs, what your strengths are, and what your goals are using Personal Par. You really must look closely at the situation and see how often the course gives you the opportunity to swing away without a potential downside risk. The answer is hardly ever.

The classic example of dot-to-dot, red/yellow/green light golf is the 1987 British Open at Muirfield. Nick Faldo won the tournament with 18 pars on the final day. He never once played directly for the flag. He showed respect for the conditions and avoided disasters by playing for the centers of the greens. Faldo is the most precise ballstriker of his generation in professional golf. If it works for him, it could do wonders for your game.

One final note on this subject: When assessing the conditions, you might find that you get predominantly red lights and hardly ever get a green light. And that's exactly the point—the more red lights you get, the more you'll reel in your game and use your strengths. Over time, as your game improves, you'll get fewer red lights and more green lights. But you have to walk before you run.

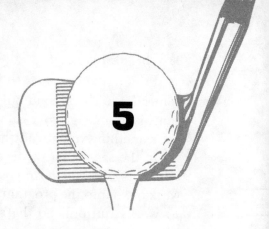

5

The Full Shots

GETTING READY IS THE MOST IMPORTANT PART

You may find it a little strange that a section on hitting the full shots appears this far into a book about how to improve your game. Especially, you might think, after a chapter that talks about how to plot your way through each hole and around the course. After all, don't you have to know how to hit full shots to employ these strategies? And don't all instruction books start out by explaining the basics? The logic for placing this subject at this point in the book goes like this: Your goal in reading this book is to break 100. We assume you're already playing the game if you're reading this book, so you already have, for better or for worse, a swing you use to hit full shots. Since this is a 13-week program, we'd like you to see improvement almost immediately. The fastest and easiest way to see strokes melt away from your game is to improve your short game; that's why that comes first. The second quickest way to knock strokes off your game is to manage your game better. That simply requires you to use something you already have—your brain.

In the sense that this is a 13-week program, improving your full shots is a long-term goal. It's something you can start on a week or so into the program and that will continue long after the 13 weeks run out. So that's the logic for placing this material here. If you were too impatient to wait for it, you probably skipped the first few chapters. If you did, go back. Patience is definitely something you need in order to break 100.

Things You Need to Know Before You Make It Go

If you were hoping for any big secrets, you'll have to wait a little while. There is a high probability that if you're struggling to break 100 you don't have a grasp of the fundamentals required to hit a shot more than 100 yards. At shorter distances you can get away with some idiosyncrasies that vary from what is considered fundamentally sound. And while it's true that some professional golfers employ techniques that include anything from flying elbows that resemble a man drinking pints at the pub (Miller Barber, Jack Nicklaus) to wild flails that look like a grandmother beating off an assailant with her umbrella (Hubert Green, Corey Pavin), you must realize that these are people who are exceptionally talented, have tremendous hand-eye coordination, and frankly, don't do much during their daylight hours other than hit golf balls. That last bit is what makes the biggest difference between you and them. And beyond that, for every example of someone who has a swing that isn't "fundamentally" sound, there are 50 examples of exceedingly fine players whose swings are fundamentally sound. (And, as you've heard the analysts on TV say time after time, the pros all get into nearly identical positions at impact. That's where all that time and repetition comes in.) The point is this: If you're not a professional golfer or a wealthy, self-employed, world-class amateur, you don't have enough free time to rely on an idiosyncratic swing to improve your ballstriking. Your only chance of developing an acceptable level of ballstriking is to understand and implement the fundamentals of swinging the club. So read on.

Give Yourself a Hand

It might seem like a statement of the obvious, but it's the place from which you must start to understand the fundamentals of striking the golf ball. The only part of your body that makes contact with the club is your hands. When you grip the club, your hands are attached to the shaft of the club, which in turn is attached to the clubhead. There are many factors that impact the angle of the clubface in relation to the ball at impact, but the predominant factor—and the one you have the most influence over—is the position of your hands on the club. Think of it this way: *Your hands are the clubface. Turn them left and the clubface rolls shut. Turn your hands to the right and the clubface opens.*

If you're a right-handed player (and all of the instruction in this book assumes you are), the placement of your left hand is the more important of the two hands. Specifically, the placement of your left thumb has tremendous influence on the position of the clubface at impact.

To determine the position of the left hand and thumb you need a point of reference. As you look down at the club when addressing the ball, mentally draw a line down the center of the front of the grip. That line is your point of reference. If your left thumb is to the left of that line, your grip will be in what is known as a weak position. The reason for the assignation of "weak" to this position is that even if you were to make a perfect swing with your left hand in this position, the clubface would be "open" (aimed right of the target) at impact. As a result, the shot would almost assuredly fly right of the target. Of the three possible grip positions (descriptions of the other two to follow), this is probably the least desirable, simply because it would produce the weakest shots—shots lacking velocity and way off target (a very "weak" shot).

If you were to place your left thumb directly down the center of that reference line your grip would be in a position that is referred to as neutral. This reflects the fact that if you were to make a perfect swing, this grip would deliver the clubface back to the ball perfectly square—aimed directly at your target. This is a perfectly fine grip if you have a perfect swing. We hope you don't think us haughty for assuming you don't have a perfect swing—but what the heck, you wouldn't be reading this book if you did. That's why we're going to recommend the third variety of grip to you.

The third variety of grip is known as a strong grip. If you position your left thumb to the right side of that reference line, you have assumed a "strong" grip. It is referred to as a strong grip because, if you make a perfect swing, it delivers the clubface to the ball slightly closed, producing a shot with maximum velocity that curves from right to left and possessing a type of spin that will make the ball run quite a bit once it hits the ground. Generally speaking, if you are having a hard time breaking 100, we can assume you could stand to hit the ball farther than you currently do. That's why this is the grip we recommend for you. There are a few *caveats*, however.

The strong grip is one of those things that feels so natural and, well, so powerful that there is a tremendous temptation to overdo it. And that is exactly what you have to guard against, because we are talking about fractions of an inch here. The easiest way to do this is to have a point of reference within your point of reference. That is to say, you need a point at which you stop turning your thumb to the right. Here's that point: When you're looking down at your grip as you address the ball, imagine you're looking at a clock. (Remember *12 O'Clock High*, when the gunners on the bombers used to shout out, "Bogey at four o'clock!" The same idea applies here—except the bogeys in your case can't kill you.) As you look down, you should position your left thumb at 1:30 on the club—the center of your thumbnail being the reference point on your thumb. Keep in mind as you do this the circumference of the clock you're visualizing. Think about it! It's not very big at all. So when you're talking about 1:30 on a clock with a circumference of approximately three inches, 1:30 is roughly 3/8 of an inch to the right of that center line. So as you can see, you really must pay attention to how much to the right of center you move your thumb. (If this whole

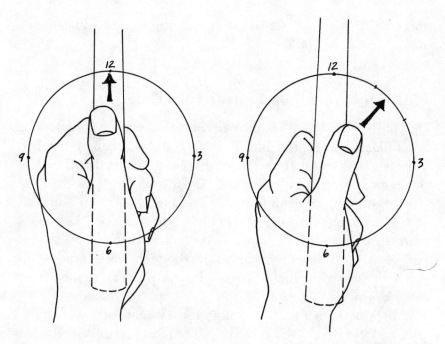

Take a stronger grip (1:30) as opposed to a neutral grip (12:00) for more consistent play.

clock thing is too confusing for you, try this: When the shaft is directly between your left thumb and the target, your grip is too strong.)

You can quite easily see the effect of moving the thumb a fraction of an inch in either direction by hitting a few balls with the thumb moved an exaggerated distance (in this case an inch-and-a-bit is exaggerated) in either direction. The shots will fly wildly off line.

Unless you are unusually talented, you'll probably want to swing the club with both hands attached to the grip of the club, which leads us to how you position your right hand on the club. And that, friend, is pretty simple. Right now, as you read this, look at your right hand. From the dead center of your wrist, visualize a straight line up into your hand. At that point of your hand, a line forms by your thumb pad when you close your hand so that your thumb reaches toward the pinkie on the same hand. That slot formed in your lower hand—that groove, if you will—

should slip over the top of your left thumb. The two hands should feel as one on the club.

Melding Your Two Hands Into One

One of the things you want to attempt to accomplish with your hand placement on the club is to get your two hands to act in unison. Comfortably fitting the right hand over the left thumb is the beginning of that process. To do this, simply place the fat pad below your right thumb over the big knuckle on your left thumb, and place your left thumb in the canal of your right palm so that your left thumb is no longer visible. The second part of that process is the relationship between the left index finger and the right pinkie finger—the two fingers nearest each other as you grip the club.

Three basic methods can marry (or not marry) these two fingers, and therefore your overall grip. The most common method of joining the left index finger and the right pinkie is typically referred to as the overlapping grip, or the Vardon grip. It's called the overlapping grip because the left pinkie finger literally lays on top of the right index finger—the left pinkie overlaps the right index finger. It is commonly referred to as the Vardon grip because its use was popularized by the great turn-of-the-century English professional Harry Vardon, who won six British Open championships.

The second manner of marrying the two fingers is what is known as the interlocking grip. With this grip, the right pinkie links between the left index finger and the left middle finger, with the tip of the left pinkie nearly touching the top of the knuckle on the left index finger. This method is probably the second most popular way of joining the hands. Coincidentally, this is the method used by history's greatest player, Jack Nicklaus, and also the type of grip used by another pretty fine player, Tom Kite. In our humble opinion, however, this is the worst of the three grips.

A hybrid method of joining the two hands is used by Greg Norman. Norman simply slides the right pinkie between the left index finger and the left middle finger. In effect, this places all 10 fingers on the club.

Norman's method of gripping the club could be described as a variation of the third (and quite uncommon) manner of gripping the club—the 10-finger grip, where the hands do not join except for the left thumb slipping under the right hand. If this type of grip—which is sometimes referred to as a baseball grip because it resembles the grip used to hold a baseball bat, with the exception of the position of the left thumb (both thumbs are off the bat in baseball)—feels comfortable to you, then you shouldn't rule it out. However, it's unlikely this grip will create the sensation of the hands working in unison. Nonetheless, there aren't many absolutes in golf, and gripping the manner in which you choose to link (or not link) your hands is a matter of personal preference. Use the grip that feels best for you.

The Aim Game: The Fine Lines

With the short iron shots described earlier, there was some emphasis on how to aim your body and, as a result, your shot. The fact is, however, that the impact of improperly aiming the club or your body on a short shot is not quite so dramatic as it is on a shot played with the longer clubs. If you misalign by as little as one inch for a full shot with your 3-wood, the result is typically a shot that is off-line by 10 yards. The longer swing and the lesser loft on the clubs you use for longer shots magnify the effect of poor alignment.

Golf is a target game, and just like any other sport that involves a target, the success of the participant depends upon the accuracy of his aim. In golf, there are two basic things that must be aimed properly in order for you to have any chance of sending the ball toward the target. The clubface must be aimed directly at your target. (Remember, the target is the point at which you want the ball to land—not necessarily where you want the ball to end up.) The second consideration in aiming is that your body must be aimed in sync with the clubface. This doesn't mean that your body is actually aimed *at* the target. *Your body stays in sync with the clubface by aiming certain key body points (especially your shoulders) along a line that is parallel to the target.*

Amazingly, one of the most common mistakes made by high handicap golfers is a failure to get the clubface aimed directly at the target. At its foundation, this is the single most important element in playing golf, but few golfers who fail to break 100 ever fully comprehend this or make it a goal—either because they don't understand it or don't pick a specific enough target, or they don't take the proper steps to get the club aimed directly at the target.

If your problem happens to be that you never fully comprehended the significance of aiming the clubface, we'll use up the rest of this sentence restating that it's *the* single most important element in hitting accurate shots. If you aren't aware of the fact that you should pick a very specific target for every shot, you should be. Even if your goal is to simply get the ball in the fairway, *you should aim at a specific spot in the fairway.* Similarly, even if your goal is to simply get the ball on the green, you should aim at a specific spot on the green. To just randomly aim your body in a general direction isn't good enough. You can't say to yourself, "I'll just aim at the fairway." It simply won't work.

The easiest way to get the clubface accurately aimed is to have a routine you go through prior to every shot. Always build your setup around your clubface. We touched on this in the short game chapter of this book, but since there's a distinct possibility you jumped to this section of the book first (or second or third) we'll cover it again—this time in more detail.

As with many things, the simplest way of getting this job done is also the best way. Almost every great player in the world aims the clubface in the following manner. No less a player than Jack Nicklaus recommends the very same routine in all his writings, teachings, and instructional videos:

- The first step is to pick your target. Let's suppose for a moment that you are on the tee and you would be content to get the ball in the fairway. Depending on the club you intend to use, make your best guess at approximately where the ball will land in terms of distance from the tee.

- Now that you have that distance in mind, from behind the ball pick a part of the fairway as your target. Depending on the ball flight of your typical shot, you may pick the left side of the fairway, the center of the fairway, or the right side of the fairway. Dividing the fairway into left, center, and right is as specific as you need to be. This will give you a target that's roughly 10 yards wide.

- Now you have a specific target in mind. Still standing behind the ball, visualize a line along the ground from the ball to your target. Then, concentrating on the area just a few inches in front of the ball along that line, pick out a "landmark"—a twig, a patch of grass that's colored a bit differently, a bit of weed, or if it's not a windy day, a stray leaf. It doesn't matter what it is; it's only important that it lie directly on the line you visualize and that once you address the ball you can see it by turning your head to the left no more than an inch.

- When you step into your setup position (which we'll cover a little farther down) you can (and should) have complete confidence in the fact that your shot is well aimed if you point the leading edge of the clubface directly at your "landmark," that intermediate target you picked out on the ground. The leading edge of the clubface is the edge at the very bottom of the clubface.

- The aiming of the lead edge must be precise. A line extending back from your intermediate target to the clubface would be perpendicular to the lead edge. This position appears "closed" or "shut" to some players and "open" to others. This is especially true for players who mistakenly use the topline of the club to aim. The only way to be precise is to be certain that a line extending back from your intermediate target is truly perpendicular to that lead edge. (It will help if you imagine the line as a thin line, perhaps the width of a pencil.)

As we said before, getting the clubface aimed is only one part of the aiming equation, but you must have a handle on that before you move on to getting your body aimed in sync. And while you go through much of the process of properly aiming the club before you address the ball, you can't actually get the club set in place until you're in the act of addressing the ball. Believe it or not, beyond getting your body lined up properly, there's actually a way of "stepping into" your setup position that will allow you to keep the clubface aimed on target and get your body set the correct way.

"Stepping Into" a Good Shot

No matter how much care you take to go through the clubface-aiming routine described above, you can screw it all up in a heartbeat if you don't get your body into the correct position. There are, of course, more lines involved here, but there's also another element: the *act* of assuming the proper body positions is just as important as the positions themselves. However, even though the act comes first, you can't execute the act without first knowing what you're trying to achieve. So first we'll cover the body positions you want to assume; then we'll tell you how to assume those positions.

If you were to imagine a line running directly from your ball to your target—and it's very important that this imaginary line is straight—such a line would serve as (and indeed be referred to as) your *target line*. This is, of course, the same line you aim the clubface along, but it's also the primary reference point for aiming your body. One of the more common mistakes made by high handicappers is that they set up to play shots believing their body should be aimed directly at the target. And that, friend, is el wrongo (a Spanish golf term meaning wrong or incorrect). When you set up to play a shot, you want your body aligned *parallel* to the target line. How exactly do you aim your body? The key point of reference is your shoulders.

A very common mental picture used to illustrate the idea of the target line and the body lines being parallel is that of a set of railroad tracks—two straight lines running very closely together and toward the same target. It's a useful image and a good one—use it if it works for you. The outside track is the target line and the inner track represents the lines you would set with your shoulders and feet.

Understanding the relationship between your body and the target line is fairly simple. As long as you understand the definition of the word "parallel," you're in business. Applying this knowledge is the part that most people screw up, and the reason for this is that rather than following a logical procedure, the average golfer just sort of walks up next to the ball and tries to get himself aligned. This creates a problem, because it is difficult to get oriented to the target when you are standing next to the ball, because your glances at the target are made by swiveling your head, and you end up assessing the situation with only one eye. Trying to orient yourself from next to the ball also creates a feeling of having to "look over" your left shoulder toward your target, which can have an impact on aligning your shoulders.

The process of getting yourself comfortably and properly situated next to the ball is actually a continuation of the process you started while getting the clubface squared to your target. It would be helpful, actually, if you were to think of the entire process of selecting a target and getting your clubface and body aligned as a *single process*, which commences the moment you step behind the ball to select your target. This is commonly referred to as a pre-shot routine, which sounds incredibly dull and academic, which is why a whole bunch of folks choose to ignore it. Don't ignore it. Call it whatever you want, but don't ignore it. Here's the entire process from apples to zinc, including the concept of "stepping into" the setup position:

- Start the process by standing directly behind the ball and selecting (first) your target and (second) your intermediate or "landmark" target on the ground a few inches ahead of the ball.

- Once you've set your targets, approach the ball, all the while eyeballing your intermediate target.

- Place your right foot *roughly* in the position you would place it in to play the shot, but don't try to set your left foot. Keep your body "open" (facing) to the target at this point.

- With your right foot set and your upper body—and more importantly, both eyes and your nose—facing the target, set the club behind the ball and get that lead edge squared to your intermediate target.

- Once you've got the clubface aimed, you can move the left side of your body into place, aligning your shoulders and feet parallel to the target line. You can also move your right foot now in order to be more comfortable.

- At this point there is a tendency to get the left shoulder pointed at the target (and therefore not parallel to the target), because now your perspective has changed—you're checking the target with your peripheral vision. Don't give into the urge to point your shoulders directly at your target. Trust your intermediate target, and remember that the idea is to keep your shoulders *parallel* to the target line. If it feels like you're aiming slightly left of the target with your shoulders, you're probably right on the money.

TERMS OF ALIGNMENT

The act of aligning yourself and the clubface accurately is arguably the most important part of hitting a golf shot—and the club hasn't even started moving yet. The aiming process is almost certainly the area of the game where the average golfer makes the most mistakes. (Even if you understand the process completely it's not difficult to start to take for granted this very important fundamental. The very fact that it's a routine can lead to mistakes—familiarity breeds contempt, or in this case, it breeds the assumption that you're doing it correctly simply because you do it often.) If you're struggling to break 100 we can guess that you're either new to the game or haven't paid much attention to the details. Part of understanding the details is knowing the language of the game, which for the most part you can pick up as you go along. However, it's essential that you get the language of the aiming process, because you're doomed to failure if you screw up the aiming process. Here are the definitions of some terms you should be familiar with:

- **Leading edge/lead edge:** A golf club has few parts but a whole bunch of sections in those parts. You can pretty much write off nearly every element of the club except the "leading edge," which is used interchangeably with "lead edge." The leading edge is the part of the clubhead where the clubface (the part that strikes the ball) and the sole (the part that rests on the ground) meet. This "edge" formed by this angle is the reference point you should use to aim the club. It's not uncommon for people to use the top line of the clubhead, but the lead edge is the part of the club closest to the ball, and therefore it is easier to be precise.

- **Target:** Your target is the place where you would like the ball to land. Be very careful to recognize the distinction between *where your ball lands and where your ball eventually comes to rest*. Let's say, for example, you decide that your ball is going to run along the ground to the right once it hits the ground. In assessing the shot, you determine that for your ball to end up where you want it to, it must land 20 yards to the left of that point. Which spot is your target: the point where the ball will first make contact with the ground, or the point where you would like it to come to rest? The answer is the former—and this is important, because it is at that point that you will aim the clubface, and in relationship to that point that you will aim your body.

- **Target line:** The target line is a straight line along the ground from the ball to your target. If you find it helpful, the line can extend past your target and also back through the ball.

- **Intermediate target:** Lying between 2 and 10 inches just ahead of your ball along the target line, the intermediate target is something you pick out while standing behind the ball. It can be a blade of grass, a discolored patch of grass, a twig, a flower—it doesn't matter as long as you can see it while you're looking down at the ball. You use it as a reference point for aiming the club, then simply connect the dots to the target.

- **Aim:** You aim one thing prior to playing a shot. You *aim* the club at your target and you align your body parallel to the target line.

- **Body:** In the sense that you align your body parallel to the target line, the word "body" refers to your shoulders and hips. Get your shoulders and hips parallel to the target line and you're in business.

WHAT HAPPENS WHEN THE LINES GET CROSSED

All this talk of lines is perhaps enough to make you dizzy. And it can get a little boring as well. The importance of all these lines, or lining up, may seem a bit clearer to you if you understand the detriment (to your score) that will result if you get your lines crossed. Here's what happens in general, although on any given swing by any given player just about anything can happen:

- If you have the clubface aimed at the target but your body is aimed left of parallel to the target line, the ball will curve from left to right. In other words, you'll hit a slice. Unless you attempt to make a compensation of some sort, there's no telling where the ball will go.

- If you have the clubface aimed at the target but your body is aimed right of parallel to the target line, the shot will curve from right to left, otherwise known as a hook.

In the above two scenarios, it's entirely possible—given the fact that you make a good swing—that your ball could end up on target. In fact, the above is exactly what you would do if you intended to hit a curving shot: Aim the clubface at your target and your body along the line on which you'd like the ball to start.

- If you get the club aimed at your target and your lower body (hips, knees, and feet) parallel to the target line, but you get your shoulders aiming *at the target (aimed right of where they should be)*, the result will be a swing that is commonly referred to as over the top, which means that when your shoulders start the downswing they don't turn level. Rather, the right shoulder gets higher or "over the top" of your left shoulder. The results run the gamut of off-line shots. This is avoidable if you have superb timing and tempo—but you're reading this book, aren't you?

- If you get the club aimed at the target, your lower body aimed at the target, and your shoulders aimed left of parallel of the target line, you'll probably either pull the ball or slice the ball.

- If you aim the clubface right of your target and aim your body left of parallel, you'll hit a slice so huge it might not stay on whichever continent you happen to be playing on at the time.

- If you aim the clubface left of the target and aim your body right of parallel, you'll hit it left of left in a big way. This will create a major league "over the top" move.

- If you aim the clubface right of the target and your body parallel to the target, you'll miss the target to the right. The ball will likely fly without much of a curve to it—what is referred to as a pushed shot.

- If you aim the clubface left of the target but get your body lined up correctly, you'll miss the target to the left—a straight-flying shot commonly known as a pull.

- If you get the club aimed correctly and your shoulders aimed parallel to the target line, but your hips, knees, and feet are pointing right of parallel, you'll take the club back too far "inside" (inside of the target line if you were to extend it back through the ball), and this, too, will result in a major "over the top" motion as you start the downswing.

- If you aim the club correctly and your shoulders are parallel to the target line, but your lower body is aimed left of parallel, it's a good bet you'll miss your target well to the right.

WHEN YOU CAN'T SEE THE TARGET

Way back before anyone reading this book was born, the Scots invented the game of golf. One of the things they thought was pretty cool was to lay out holes in a manner where a player couldn't always see where he wanted the shot to end up. This is known as a blind shot, and depending on whom you're speaking with, they are either really fun to play or they are "tricked up" and take away any advantage a skilled player might have. (By the way, don't blame the Scots for these holes—they were just using the land as they found it.) Regardless of your opinion of blind shots, however, you've got to deal with these shots when confronted with them, unless you just decide to walk off the course. So what do you do when you can't see where your ball is going to land? After all, you have to have a target in mind if you're to aim properly, right? Here's what you do:

- If you haven't played the course before, ask the people you're playing with if any of them are familiar with the hole. If they are, ask them for a landmark at which you can aim and then go about the business of determining an intermediate target (a few inches ahead of your ball, on a straight line between the ball and the landmark), so you can get yourself properly aimed. Be certain to ascertain any key distance factors from the knowing individual(s) as well, so you know which club you should use.

- If no one you're playing with is familiar with the hole, you have two options: You can go scout out the hole, or you can wing it. The first option is really only a realistic option if you are using a motorized cart and the pace of play is rather slow. (Unfortunately on both counts, this isn't all that unusual.) However, if play is moving along and you're playing on foot, we can't recommend you walk ahead to check things out, considering the fact that the players behind you may consider lynching you if you do so. If play is slow, however, take advantage of that fact and check things out. If you decide to wing it—that is, to simply make a guess as to where to play the shot—make sure after the shot that you stop on the way to the ball at the point where you can see what should have been your target and still see the spot from which you played the shot. Make a mental note of some landmark that you can use as an aiming point next time you play the hole.

• Playing a blind shot is very similar to the choosing of and aligning to the intermediate target you use on a normal shot, except in this case you're selecting a surrogate target if you will. Typically, when playing a blind hole, your best bet for an aiming point is a tall (real tall) tree that can be seen over whatever hill is rising up (or dropping down) in front of you. Obviously, you can't just pick out any tall tree—it has to lie on an extension of the target line beyond the actual target. If on the outside chance you're playing a links (seaside) course and it doesn't have any trees but it does have lots of blind holes, you should take a caddie if one is available.

Keeping Your Feet Firmly on the Ground

If you look closely at the feet of any famous golfers at address, either in still photos or on TV or in person, you'll notice something fairly quickly—their feet aren't *perpendicular* to the target line. Perhaps this might strike you as odd considering all the time we've spent talking about how your feet should be *parallel* to the target line. After all, it only makes sense that you would use the tips of your shoes as the reference point for aligning your feet, and if a line across the tips of your shoes was supposed to be parallel to another line (the target line), then it would also make sense that the shoe tips themselves would be perpendicular to that line. The fact, however, is that you would find it incredibly difficult to swing if your feet were perpendicular to the target line—you'd either fall over or put a tremendous amount of strain on your knees.

When it comes to your feet there are three things you should be thinking about when you set up to the ball: where they're aligned, how they're positioned, and how far apart they are.

We've covered the aligning part in depth earlier, but the position-ing part goes hand in hand with the aligning part. As noted above, there might be some confusion about exactly what posi-tion your feet should be in at address, and by that we mean where the tips of your shoes should be pointing.

The movement of the club in golf consists of two body turns: one turn back and one turn forward. If you stand with the tip of your right shoe perpendicular to the target line, you won't be able to turn back as far as you should. That's why we're going to give you the following bit of advice: *By flaring open your right foot you make it possible to complete your backswing turn and to achieve all the good things that occur as a result.* By "flaring open" we're talking about pointing the tip of your right shoe slightly to your right. For example, if you were standing in the middle of giant clock you might point the tip of your shoe between the 12 and the 2. That might not seem like much, but you will certainly notice the difference if you turn your foot out just that little bit.

And what about your left foot? You'll want to flare out the toe of it as well, to about the 11 on the big clock. This will help you keep your balance, especially when the left leg takes on the full weight and force of impact (as you'll see in the next chapter).

At this point it is worth remembering that for a fundamen-tally sound setup, your feet should be parallel to the target line. To get your reference point, you can still run that imaginary line along the tips of your shoes—even though they are flared out, that imaginary line should still be a straight line.

How Wide Is Wide Enough, but Not Too Wide

The third matter of relevance relating to your feet in the setup position is the distance between the right foot and the left foot. This is commonly referred to as your stance width. This is one of those things we can't give you precise advice on, because every-one has a different body and everyone has a different sense of what feels balanced. What we can do is explain the effect stance width has on your swing and give you some parameters.

The distance between your feet also affects the amount you can turn your body and the balance you need to maintain while doing so. If you get your feet too close together it will impact most on your balance. You'll be able to turn, but you won't be able to generate any power. If you get your feet too far apart it will affect your ability to turn. You'll have plenty of balance and a proper base—you'll also feel like the Tin Man when you swing. (The Tin Man before the oil, that is.)

So how far apart should your feet be? Here's the general rule: For a full shot, they should be no narrower than hip width and no wider than shoulder width. That, of course, brings a few variables into play: namely, what is your point of reference for your feet and shoulders. (There shouldn't be any confusion about where exactly your hips begin and end. If there is, use your hip sockets as your reference point.) For your feet, you should use the middle of your heels as your measuring point, and for your shoulders you would use your shoulder socket (that's the part where your arm connects to your torso). So using those guidelines, here are some revised rules:

- The distance between the centers of your heels should never be narrower than the distance between your hips.

- The distance between the centers of your heels should never be wider than the distance between your shoulder sockets when you're standing straight up—not when you're addressing the ball.

Using these guidelines doesn't leave much room for variation—the distance between your hips and the distance between your shoulder sockets could hardly be considered significant. But it is. A matter of a half-inch or so could make a difference in your swing, so it's a good idea to experiment a bit. A good general rule to go by is this: *At the end of a balanced swing, when you've turned your upper body toward the target, your knees should almost touch each other.* If they don't, your stance is too wide. If they do, but you feel some strain in your right knee, your stance might be too narrow.

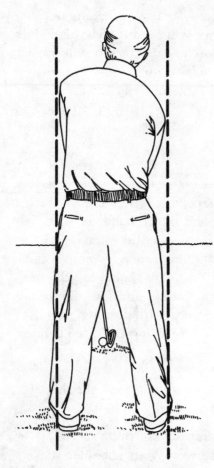

Stance width should be as wide as the outside of your shoulders.

This golfer's stance is too narrow. It will be difficult for him to maintain proper balance on either the takeaway or the downswing.

Posture: Momma Always Warned You About Your Posture—and She Was Right

Remember when you were a kid and your parents were always saying things such as "Watch your posture" and "Sit up straight" and "Pull your shoulders back" and "Quit slouching like that; you look like a _____." Is it possible that they knew some day you'd be on a quest to break 100 and that your posture would have something to do with whether you succeeded or failed in this quest? It's nice to think so, but they probably just wanted you to get your face out of your cereal bowl. But just in case you thought that once you were out of the fifth grade you'd never again have to listen to someone make reference to your posture, guess again.

Your posture at address (and throughout your swing) isn't typically considered one of the basic fundamentals of the game, but it should be. The litany of problems created by poor posture is as long as that of any other failed fundamental in golf.

When we talk about posture in golf, we're really talking about how you lower the clubhead and yourself into position to play a shot. If you stood straight up, the club wouldn't reach down to the ball, and if you slouched over too far, you'd stick the club into the ground out beyond the ball and behind it. These are extreme examples, of course, but if you back them up a little bit, you can see the importance of posture.

The basic fundamental posture for a good golf swing is the same as that for nearly any other sport. If you visualize the "ready" position that athletes assume just prior to action, it's very similar from sport to sport. Run these images through your mind:

- A professional tennis player waiting to return serve.

- A professional basketball player preparing to shoot a foul shot.

- An NFL quarterback waiting to take the snap of the football.

- A hockey goalie waiting for a shot to be played at him.

- A batter waiting on a pitch.

What do all these images have in common? For starters, the knees are slightly flexed. Second, the upper body is tipped forward from the hips. Third, the arms are relaxed. Okay, those are sort of obvious. Here's two more things they have in common: First, if you were to look at this person from the side, you could draw a line from the balls of their feet, through the tips of their knees, through the tips of their elbows, and up through their shoulder sockets. The line would be nearly straight. The point is that these key points—the balls of the feet, the knees, the elbows, and the shoulders are all stacked on top of each other. The final commonality is this: These athletes are all *ready to respond*. And while you may not need to respond to someone else in golf—you initiate and exert complete control over the action—you do need to be ready to respond to your brain when it says, "Okay, start swinging." That's why you need to set your posture at address and maintain it throughout your swing.

Since it's tough for you to check if all those key points are lined up, we're going to suggest two ways for you to find your ideal posture at address. Here's the first:

- Standing straight up, and without a club, place your hands on your thighs.

- Now bend forward from your hips and lower yourself with your knees, just as if you were sitting on the edge of a stool.

- When the tips of your fingers reach the tops of your knees, that's the position you want.

Here's another way to become familiar with proper posture:

- Holding a club, extend your arms directly out in front of you and point the club straight out, too, as if it were an extension of your arms.

- Cocking your wrists, lift the club toward the sky until it is at a 45 degree angle to your body.

- Drop your arms toward your chest until the back of your arm touches your chest.

- Now lower your hands until the butt of the club is pointing perpendicular to your spine and at your belly button.

- Now tilt forward from your hips and down with your knees until the club is soled on the ground.

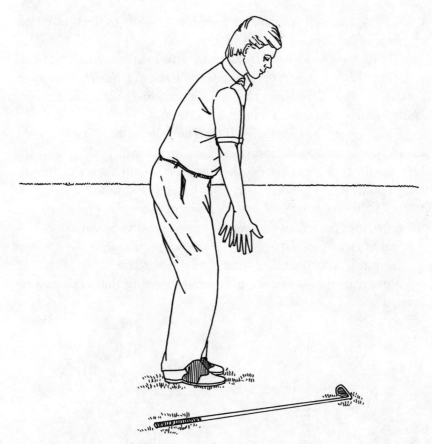

To find proper posture, bend forward from the hips and back at the knees and slide your hands down until they touch the tops of your knees. This should feel like sitting on a stool.

- Once you've soled the club, hold it in that position and make a practice hip turn. There should be enough room for your hip to turn through the ball without hitting the butt of the club.

Ball Position

The position of the ball in relation to your body is the final key element of your setup. Because the club swings in an arc, it has an optimum point of impact—a millisecond of time and space when the club stops moving down and starts moving up. If you don't have the ball positioned to coincide with that point of the clubhead's arc, you've got problems.

There are two points to keep in mind on the matter of ball position: *First, your reference point is not its position between your feet. You determine the ball's position in relation to your chest—more precisely, the center of your chest.*

The second key point is this: There may be a time in the future, as your game improves, that you'll want to change the ball position depending on the shot you want to play and the club you're hitting. For the moment, keep it simple by adhering to this rule: *Keep the ball one inch left of your chest for every full iron shot and fairway wood played off the ground. For a driver or a teed up fairway wood, play the ball off your left armpit. For a short iron or pitch, play it in the center of your chest.*

Now turn the page and learn how to swing that club and hit it hard.

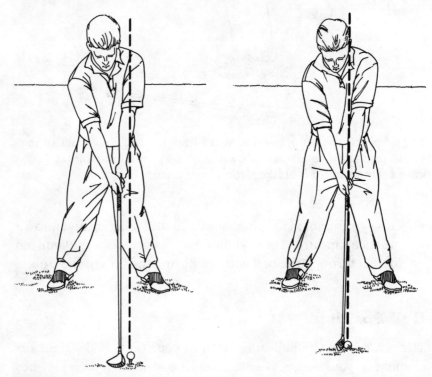

Proper ball position for the driver, fairway woods, and long irons.

Proper ball position for the short irons.

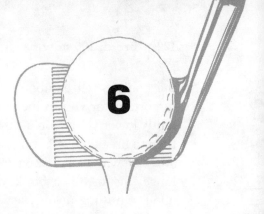

6

Swinging for Power

YOU SWING THE CLUB AND THE CLUB (NOT YOU!) HITS THE BALL

If you were to take a poll of every golfer in the world, both amateurs and professionals, tournament players and all-time legends, they'd all say they would like to hit the ball farther. For many golfers, the quest to hit the ball farther is merely a matter of being greedy or wanting to soothe their egos. In your case (that of a golfer struggling to break 100), the yearning for added power in your game is born of necessity. For the long-term improvement of your game and to consistently lower your average scores, you need to hit the ball longer than you currently do. We know from experience at our schools that if we take high handicap golfers and let them play from our own drives, they have no problem breaking 100. On the other hand, if we play from their drives, our own scores are significantly higher than normal.

It would make sense if you were thinking at this point: If this is so damned important, why did these guys wait until this far into the book to tell us about it? The answer is that while it is very important for you to increase the length of your shots to consistently lower your scores—that is to say not only to break 100, but then to break 90 and eventually, perhaps, to break 80—it is not the *quickest* way to knock strokes off your game. Hitting the ball a longer distance is a big key to lower scores, but breaking 100 is about whittling away wasted strokes—the kind you fritter away around the greens and from the sand and through mental mistakes. And those are the easiest things to fix and show the quickest results.

Hitting for distance takes the longest time to learn because the full swing is, mechanically speaking, the longest part of the game—it has the most room for mistakes and requires more understanding of what you're attempting to do. It's very difficult to learn to hit the ball farther if you don't understand what goes into creating the power that sends that ball flying. (It's true that some people have a knack for hitting the ball a long way without trying or really understanding why. We can assume you're not one of those people if you're reading this book.) Having said that, we'll get the ball rolling (or should we say flying) with a nuts-and-bolts explanation of what creates power in the golf swing.

Don't Look Now, but You're a Giant Spring

To hit the ball with any semblance of power you must understand the idea of "coiling" your body. Think of it this way: Your body in motion as you prepare to hit a golf ball is a giant spring. As you turn the top of your body back away from the ball, the lower body resists and the spring is tightening—it is storing up energy, which turns into power. Like any other spring, it reaches a point of maximum tautness and it can't get any tighter. The only thing that can happen then is that the spring releases. And when a fully coiled spring releases when it is fully wound it doesn't release gently—it explodes. That's the basic idea behind hitting the ball a long way. So think of yourself as a spring, and the action of tightening this spring as "coiling."

For a spring to coil (and for your body to coil), there has to be some resistance. An actual spring, for instance, is anchored on one end (the fixed end) and the other end (the drive end) winds against that resistance. In your swing, your feet and knees act as the fixed end of the spring during your backswing. The rest of your body (the drive end of the spring) turns around that base, and the farther a body part is from the fixed end the farther it has to turn to get wound as tight as possible. In plain talk, that means that your hips turn back a certain amount, but your shoulders turn back even farther, because they are farther away from the fixed end (your base).

Okay, now your spring is fully wound and it's time for it to "uncoil" or release its energy. Where do you suppose the maximum amount of energy is stored in that spring? Is it out at the far end of the coil, which in this case would be your hands? Or would it be at the core of the spring, the part closest to the fixed end (in this case that would be your hips, which are closest to the fixed point, your base)? The answer is, the part of your body closest to the fixed point. Since your hips have the maximum of energy stored up, that's the point at which the energy starts to uncoil. In other words, the downward part of the swing begins with your hips. The maximum *effect (maximum speed)*, however, is seen at the far end of the coil, i.e., your hands, which happen to be attached to the club, which is even farther away from your hips. When you include the club, the point farthest from your hips is the clubhead. And that's the point where the maximum amount of speed is generated. And the front of the clubhead (the clubface) is what collides with the ball. So the faster that clubhead is moving, the farther the ball flies. And the tighter your body coils, the faster that clubhead will move—as long as you uncoil in the proper sequence, which isn't automatic, since your body isn't actually a spring, and a spring doesn't have a brain screaming "Kill it!" as it swings a club. But at least now you understand the theory behind the power production. Now we can get to the practical application of it.

Okay, So You're Not a Spring—but Work With Us Here. We Promise You'll Understand It.

We know that the above sounds a little complex, even though we did our best to make it seem harmless. But we promise that understanding it will take you a long way toward hitting the ball farther. And while there may be a bit more theory and the odd metaphor here and there along the way, we'll try to keep it as simple as possible from here on in.

At some point after running through your mental checklist of things to do before you actually start to move the club, your brain will say, "Okay, start moving the club." What do you do when that instinct kicks in? What starts to move first?

If you'll permit us another reference to the spring, it would be helpful. While it is the fixed end (your base) that stores up the energy, you cannot wind the spring from the fixed end. To wind the spring you have to start from the drive end (the farthest end from the fixed end) and begin twisting. As noted above, the drive end of your "body spring" is your arms and, by extension, your hands and the club. So your arms start the movement in the backswing, and as they swing across your chest, your right hip simultaneously turns back over your right heel to establish the lower body pivot.

When your arms begin the movement away from the ball, they are "swinging" away from the ball, i.e., they are moving like a pendulum until the moment that your hips start to turn. Once those hips start moving, something else starts to move—your shoulders. You can try it right now: Stand up and turn your hips to the right. Can't do it without your shoulders turning, can you? While you're up, let's try that entire sequence. Get yourself in that perfect posture position we described to you in the last chapter (remember, pretend you're sitting on a stool). Okay, now hang your arms down and keep them real loose. (Think of an Olympic swimmer on the blocks prior to a race. Visualize the way they wiggle their arms to keep them loose. That's how your arms should feel.) Start swinging your arms back and forth. You'll notice when your arms are swinging to the right that your hips will start to turn with them. And once your hips start to turn and your arm starts to swing across your chest, your shoulders will go along for the ride. That's how things get going in your backswing.

For Every Swing, Turn, Turn, Turn. There Is a Reason to Turn, Turn, Turn.

If you weren't playing golf you probably wouldn't give much thought to the idea of "turning" your body. Sure, you might "turn" your head in everyday life, and you might "turn around" to see something, but very seldom would you attempt to "turn your body" around itself, with your feet remaining in the same position. So let's talk a little bit about the idea of turning your body in the context of the golf swing.

There are people who would go so far as to say the golf swing consists of two movements: a turn back (away from the ball) and a turn through (toward and through the ball). Frankly speaking, for a golfer of your current skill level, this isn't a bad way of regarding of the full swing. It may seem a bit simplistic, but it will hold you in good stead and really does put you in touch with the basic power source for any golfer.

Here's a checklist to get the power in your game "turned on":

- **To begin your backswing, think about swinging your arms and turning your right hip back away from the ball.** By using your right hip as your mark, you'll almost assuredly shift your weight over your right heel. And that's perfect! That's the fixed point you turn around.

- **Your shoulders have already started moving by now, and they act as your next mark. When your shoulders feel as if they can't turn back any farther, you've completed your backswing.** Don't worry about whether the club has reached "parallel" (a point where it is parallel to the ground) as you might have heard on TV or read elsewhere. That is really not a goal of your backswing. It's simply a reference point good players use to see if they are overswinging. Getting the club parallel with the ground is not a significant contributor to any golfer's game. A useful reference point, if you can do it, is to get your left shoulder somewhere in the vicinity of your chin and behind the ball.

- **Once you've completed your backswing, you've reached a very crucial moment in your swing—a moment when a lot of things can blow up in your face in a split second.** Here's why: Once the top of the swing has been reached, the most common impulse is to rip the arms and/or hands forward toward the ball. This is one of those impulses you must resist. To create any power at all in your swing, you must start the downswing with your arms (dropping the club down—not forward) and your hips. Specifically, turn your left hip over your left heel and toward your target, and don't stop until you've completely followed through on the shot. By using the left hip as your mark, you'll get your weight shifted into your left leg for the downswing, and your left leg acts as your fixed point for your spring as you start the downswing.

- **One final point about turning: You must strive to achieve a "level" turn.** What does that mean? Simply put, you should strive for a feeling that your hips are turning level with the ground throughout your swing. By keying on turning your hips level to the ground, you'll avoid tipping toward the target or away from the target, both of which will cause you some serious trouble.

One of the great learning images of all time was given to golfers back in the early part of the 20th century by the legendary teacher Percy Boomer, and it still holds true today. Boomer realized the importance of the hips turning level with the ground and as such advised his students (and those who read his writings) to think of the swing as "turning in a barrel." Boomer understood that it might be difficult for you to make the connection between your hips and the ground, so he came up with this bit of imagery that would allow you to compare the progress of your turning hips to the top circumference of a barrel if you were standing inside that barrel when you made your swing. The top of the barrel (back in his day, he was talking about the wooden-type barrel) when stood on end (and with the lid removed) came right up to the hips.

DON'T LOSE IT AT THE TOP

The point at which the club stops moving away from the ball and starts moving back toward the ball is referred to as the "top" of your swing. Aside from the initial setup position, this is the phase of the game where the most errors occur for the average golfer.

To understand why, it helps to make a distinction between "swinging" the club and "hitting at" the ball. The distinction is easy to make in your mind; it's just hard to get yourself to do it. The basic idea is this: You shouldn't think of golf as an attempt by you to hit the ball. *You swing the club and the club hits the ball. Repeat: You don't hit the ball—the club does.* What makes this tough to act upon is the impulse you feel at the top to lash out at the ball with your hands/arms. Have you ever been at a fair or carnival and watched a real big guy swing the mallet to try and ring the bell—and he doesn't even come close? That's because he swung with only his arms instead of using his body in conjunction with his arms. The same thing will happen to you if you start the downswing with your hands and arms moving forward (instead of down) once you get to the top of your swing—it will feel powerful, but it won't be delivering true power, because you'll be unwinding your "body spring" from the wrong end. And when you do that, all the power escapes unused.

An extremely common mistake among golfers at all levels (even the very best) is a move that's known as swinging over the top, which refers to what happens when you start the downswing with your upper body—that is, your right shoulder gets "over" your left as it moves out toward the target line; the club gets "over" the plane on which it should be moving. "Over the top" is not a good thing. It causes an array of weak, off-line shots (wild slices, pulls, duck hooks), all of which at their root have one thing in common: a downswing started with the upper body.

If you have any golf videos at home that feature tour players, watch them make a swing at the slowest possible speed setting on your VCR. If you can see the swing clearly at a slow speed you will notice something amazing: The golfer's hips will actually start turning toward the target while his shoulders *are still turning back away from the target.* That's a tremendous example of how important it is for your hips to lead the downswing, but it's not something you want to attempt to copy. Something you may want to copy from a terrific tour player can be seen in the swing of Nancy Lopez, who has a well-known trademark: an apparent "pause" at the top of the swing. During this pause, the club seems to hang in suspended animation for a second or two—long enough that even the most novice observer would notice the length of time for which the club seems motionless. But while it may appear that Lopez has come to a complete stop, only her upper body has paused momentarily—just long enough to let her hips get a head start on the way down. Another player you can see this in to a somewhat lesser extent is Senior PGA Tour player and longtime amateur standout Jay Sigel.

Even if you decide it just isn't your style to try to copy Lopez or Sigel, you might find that just the *idea* of a pause at the top will help you achieve your goal during this transitional phase of your swing. Thinking about a pause will plant the seed that you shouldn't be in any hurry to get the downswing started. When you think that way—and give your body a chance to do its thing—good things will happen.

The Power Within You Unleashed: Patience Will Get You There, Friend

By now you have a pretty good idea of how to store up power in your backswing and how to initiate your downswing. Truth be known, those are the two biggies when it comes to generating distance. At least they are the major points that most golfers fail to understand and therefore fail to accomplish. They aren't the only things you need to know, however. Once you start the club down you have to finish the swing.

The best and simplest swing thought to start your downswing is to turn your left hip (or if you prefer, your left trouser pocket) behind you (toward the target) as much as you do when you throw a baseball. Once you do this, you'll get your weight shifted into your left leg, which will provide something for you to unwind against, and your upper body (shoulders, arms, hands, and the club) will follow the lead of the lower body. Everything will be moving in the proper sequence, and assuming you set up to the ball in a fundamentally sound manner, you'll be in position to hit a super shot.

Up until now this idea of hitting longer shots is calling upon you to exercise more patience than you are probably used to when swinging the golf club—or doing much of anything else for that matter. It takes tremendous patience to "wait on" your swing at the top. On your way down to the ball your patience is challenged even farther still, because if you try to hurry things along at any time, you'll screw up the sequence of body movements. Is it possible there might be some way to alleviate the need to feel as if you have to "hurry up" to hit the ball? For instance, what if you were to disregard the ball in a manner of speaking, that is, make your goal to swing the club to the finish position rather than striking the ball? Sound a little crazy? A little too far out there for a logical person such as yourself?

Remember back in the short game chapter when we talked about how important it was to follow through on every shot from the sand? Well, the sand isn't the only place where the follow-through is important. The follow-through plays a vital role in every shot you play, including putts, with the exception of a few specialty shots in the short game. Completing every swing to a full follow-through position—be it a tee shot, a 6-iron, or a 30-foot putt—assures that the clubhead will continue to pick up speed (whatever that speed may be) through impact with the ball. This is a critical element in hitting on-target shots, because if the clubhead slows down through the ball, the clubface will almost always twist open or closed. An off-line shot is the result.

Since the follow-through is so important to begin with, what if you used the completion of it as your second goal in a two-thought swing process consisting of these two thoughts: (1) Swing your arms across your chest as you turn away from the ball level, and (2) swing through to your finish position, starting down with your hips just as if you were making an underhand throw toward the target.

By focusing on these two thoughts, you can accomplish two things: namely, get the sequence of movements in order and remove the bashing of the ball as your goal. You might find it a whole lot easier to be patient if contact with the ball isn't your ultimate goal. The follow-through position is a little less dramatic than the collision of impact, so you don't need to be in any hurry to get there—it'll still be waiting for you when you arrive.

If it helps at all, try visualizing the pros on TV. Watch them swing through to the finish position: weight on the left foot; hips and shoulders turned toward the target; hands up somewhere between the left ear and left shoulder; club hanging across the back. We aren't the first teachers to say the following, and we certainly won't be the last: If you swing the club through to that Tour player TV finish, you'll do an amazing number of things correct before you reach that point—one of them being the launch of a respectable golf shot. Instead of looking at your downswing as the means to an end (hitting the ball), you might be better served thinking about the end (a full follow-through) creating the means (a good swing). The flight of the ball itself is neither "means" nor "end." It just happens.

Tempo: Moderating the Power You Create

If you were driving a car with an extremely powerful engine, common sense would tell you that it wasn't advisable to keep the accelerator nailed to the floor. For starters it would be dangerous, and it probably wouldn't be the best thing in the world for the engine, either. Similarly, if you were to alternately depress the accelerator and then let off it, and you did this continually, two things would happen: You would have reduced control over the car's performance, and you would never recognize any of the benefits of the powerful engine, such as a smooth, effortless ride.

As you've almost certainly ascertained by now, the analogy above applies to your golf swing as well. And the word most commonly used in golf to describe the application of power and the consistency of that application is *tempo*. Think about that term for a second: *tempo*. What does that mean to you right this very second? There's a fairly high likelihood that to you "tempo" means "swing slow." After all, when your know-it-all friends are bombarding you with well-intended but worthless advice, the first two suggestions are (1) "Keep your head down/keep your eye on the ball," and (2) "Slow it [your swing] down. You're swinging way too fast, partner."

With regard to the latter of these two common bits of advice and/or encouragement, there is something very telling that prevents it from being completely worthless: There is indeed something that appears to be moving too fast to your friendly observer. What your friend sees is a jolting change in the *tempo* of your swing. Not the speed, mind you, but the tempo. The tempo of your swing and the speed of your swing *are* related, but they do not mean the same thing. And to the extent that you have control over either of them, tempo is the more important of the two. *Tempo* is the consistency of the pace at which the club is moving. *Clubhead speed* is how fast the club is moving at any given microsecond. Ideally, you want the clubhead speed to reach its maximum at impact, but that can happen only if you keep your engine under control. That is to say, you're only going to achieve maximum clubhead speed at impact if you moderate the tempo of the movements of your body.

This concept might raise the following question in your mind: If you move your body at the same tempo throughout the swing, how is the club going to steadily gain speed? That's a logical question, so we'll use a logical image: Let's say you took a piece of string and tied it to a washer. (Not the kind of washer you clean your clothes in—the small, circular things with a hole in the middle that help keep screws tight and faucets from leaking.) Okay, now let's say you tie the other end of the string to your finger, snug enough that you'll be able to start spinning the washer around your finger. Now start moving your finger in a circular motion. Pretty soon, without changing the pace at which you move your finger, the washer will start spinning around your finger—slowly at first, but gaining speed all the time. The steadier the finger is (not flapping wildly about) and the more consistent the tempo of the finger, the faster that washer will go. In other words, the washer gains speed based on the constant pace of your finger and the fact that it's not at the center of the power source, but rather as far away as possible from the power source.

You should be able to see where this is going: In this analogy, the finger is your hips and the washer is the clubhead of the club you are swinging. It follows, then, that the tighter and more evenly paced your turn and coil, the faster that clubhead will be moving at impact. *But the clubhead doesn't start out moving at maximum speed; it picks up speed as it travels. If it starts out too quickly or too out of control, it can't gain speed. If the consistency of your body swing tempo is broken at any point during the swing, the clubhead will lose whatever momentum it has built up.*

So how do you keep tabs on the tempo of your body swing? Here are a few rules to keep in mind:

- A lot depends on what occurs during the first 18 inches or so of your backswing. If you start the club back slowly, you're in good shape. If you whip the club away from the ball as if you're about to beat off an attacker, you're dead. You'll never be able to gain control of the club during the swing. So here's a thought to get you started: *low and slow.* It's easy to remember (it's only three words and it rhymes—what more could you ask for), and all it means is to keep the club "low" to the ground for the first 18 inches or so (your nice, level turn will take care of that) and to take it back under control.

- Once again, a crucial moment occurs at the "top" of your swing, when there is a tremendous urge to "hit at the ball." Not only does this affect the sequence of body movements as described earlier (by lashing at the ball with the arms), but it also creates a desire to "speed things up." Leading with the lower body is a huge help in avoiding this. Another way to facilitate a smooth transition from backswing to downswing without disrupting your tempo is to think of the swing in terms of a ballroom-type dance tempo: one. . . two. . . three. . . . one. . . two. . . three. . . . one. . . two. . . three,. . . etc. You start the swing (one); you transition the swing (two); and you swing through the ball (three).

- Remember that "tempo" refers to your body, "speed" refers to the clubhead. *While you're swinging you simply cannot concern yourself with thoughts related to how fast the club-*

head is traveling. If you want clubhead speed, monitor the tempo of your body and forget about the club.

TEMPO: YOU'VE GOT TO WALK YOUR WALK

In the minds of a lot of people the words "tempo" and "smooth" equate to "slow." If that is your perception of tempo, you might wonder why some professional tour golfers (Tom Watson, for example) apparently swing very quickly, while others (let's say Lee Janzen) seem to swing at a rather modest pace? How can there be such an obvious difference in the pace of the swings of two world-class golfers? And what's with Watson? Hasn't he read any of this tempo stuff?

There's no question that the pace of Watson's swing is much quicker than that of Lee Janzen's, but both golfers swing with superb tempo. Would it help Watson to "slow down" his swing? Absolutely not. Watson's upbeat tempo is an extension of the way he does things in life. Watch him walk the fairways of a golf course and you'll notice that he walks along at a pretty good clip. He makes quick decisions, too. You see other players languishing over the ball as if the future of mankind depended on their club selection. Watson takes a look and grabs a club.

Think of some more players: Greg Norman strides along rather briskly; Fuzzy Zoeller lolls along as if he forgot he had somewhere to go. Freddie Couples just sort of glides down the fairways; Lee Trevino walks like he has ants in his pants. Their swings all match the way they walk. When the swing tempo doesn't match up with the walk, they've got problems.

So what does all this mean to you? Just like all the fine players mentioned above, the pace of your swing should reflect the pace at which you normally walk. If you walk fast, the tempo of your swing should match that. If you walk slow, the tempo should match that. If you walk quickly, this doesn't mean you have an excuse to swing out of control—it simply means it's okay to feel as if your swing is briskly paced. The key is that it should feel that way from the start.

And if you're a brisk swinger, what about that tip above that advised you to think "low and slow" in the takeaway. That's simple: *It's whatever feels slow to you.* Your idea of slow and someone else's idea of slow are always going to be two different things. Just worry about your own sense of feel. After all, you're the only one who knows how that feels.

Super Power Tips

Up until this point in this book we've been providing you with easy-to-understand, easy-to-implement advice on how to hit full shots and how to increase your power production. But we're not stupid (no matter what our spouses say), and we know you and every other golfer would like some top secret tips on how to hit it long. Real long. Super long. Tiger Woods long. Cannon-shot long. Sorry to disappoint you, bub, but there aren't any top secret we'd-have-to-kill-you-if-we-told-you type tips on how to hit longer drives. Be that as it may, here's a few tips on how to squeeze the last few yards out of any shot and become "sneaky" long. You must remember two things: It's never a good idea to take an entire bottle of medicine at once. Golf tips are the same way. Second, all of these suggestions have a point of diminishing return—they're good to a certain point, then they become a detriment to your end goal. And trust us, that point comes a lot sooner than you expect it to.

- **Don't try to hit it hard.** Sounds simple, perhaps even stupid. But if you stand on the tee and say to yourself "I'm gonna whomp this one," it isn't going to happen. The best way to whomp one is to pick a swing key and zone in on it. Forcing the club toward the ball almost always results in an off-center hit.

- **Grip it and let it rip itself.** In the previous chapter we mentioned the position of your left thumb as being at 1:30. Well, the farther to right of the club you move that thumb, the more the club will close through impact. Up to a certain point (depending mostly on the rest of your fundamentals and mechanics) this can help you hit shots that curve from right to left (a draw). This type of shot, if you can control it, will run farther than a straight shot or one that curves from left to right. Of course, it won't run anywhere if you turn your hand so far under that you drive the ball straight into the ground. On your grip "clock," 2:30 would be an absolute maximum to try. You'll be amazed at the difference between 1:30 and 2:00.

- **Over the line of fire.** In the last chapter we went to some length to advise you on how to keep your body aligned parallel to the target line. To get the maximum distance out of any shot, you want to get that sucker curving from right to left. The best way to do that without losing control is to get the clubhead moving toward the ball on a *slightly* more inside tack than it would take if you lined up in a fundamentally square position. To do this you still want to picture that line that runs parallel to your target line. However, rather than aiming your key body points along that line, you can try getting those key body lines (feet, knees, hips, and shoulders) aimed just to the right of that line (try about an inch for starters) while keeping the clubface squared to the target. The body lines should still line up, so your body can move in the proper sequence, but they aren't parallel to the target line. The above produces a *slightly* closed stance, and it does two things: It programs a swing path that will bring the clubhead to the ball more from farther inside the target line, promoting a draw. Second, it will place your right foot in a position drawn farther back from the target line. This will allow your hips and, as a result, your shoulders to turn even farther away from the ball. If you've been reading closely, you know that creates more power.

- **Get aggressive with your hips.** Adjusting your grip as described above also provides you with another benefit. Simply speaking, the gas pedal for your clubhead speed is the winding and unwinding of your hips. The faster they unwind, the faster that clubhead is going to be moving. There's a bit of danger, however, if your hips get going too fast and your grip is more neutral than strong. The danger, unless you have extraordinary timing, is that the club won't have a chance to get itself squared to the target prior to impact and you'll hit a shot *way* right. With the strong grip and the nearly guaranteed slightly closed/square clubface at address, you can get very aggressive with your lower body. If you really want to nail one, when you get to the top of your swing think: "Fire!" Then whoosh that right hip toward your target.

- **Check to see where your feet are pointing.** Remember in the last chapter we recommended flaring out your feet? By pointing your right foot toward the right and combining it with the closed stance, you'll be able to make the biggest possible turn away from the ball. Turning your left foot out will help that leg straighten in the downswing, which is what causes all that energy you built up to be transferred to the clubhead.

- **Keep both feet on the ground.** As the weight shifts from the right side to the left side in the downswing there exists a tendency among some golfers to lift the right foot off the ground—specifically the right heel. This prematurely lets power leak out of your swing without being used. To turn through your shot, however, you do need to make some adjustment in your right foot as you move through the ball. Rather than getting the foot up on its toe, think about "rolling" onto the inside of your right foot so that the entire length of the foot stays in contact with the ground.

- **When things go bad, go back to basics.** Remember that while hitting the ball a long way is fun, it's not worth any toll you have to pay in accuracy. If you try these power tips and the ball starts flying all over the place, go back to basics—forget the strongest grip, the closed stance, the long driver, and everything else. Just line up square to the target line and start hitting some fairways again.

THE TOP FIVE POWER LEAKS

If it sounds like it's easy to generate power, it's even easier to do things that create "power leaks" or moves that greatly inhibit your chances of producing your maximum distance. Here's a list of the five most common power killers—the things that'll leave you wanting more.

1. **You're squeezing the life out of your club.** Your body's ability to turn and the club's ability to react to your body are heavily dependent upon an almost complete lack of physical tension while you set up to a shot and while swinging. The single biggest cause of overall body tension (at least as it relates to golf) resides in your hands. Specifically, the amount of pressure you apply to the club with your hands (grip pressure) plays a major role in determining how well your body complies with the demands you place upon it. Try it right now. Place your hands together as if you were going to grip a club. Now squeeze them as hard as you can. Feel that tension in your lower arms? Upper arms? Chest? Maybe even your abdominal muscles? Think your body is going to be able to achieve maximum coil with all that going on? Not a chance. Remember, a spring slowly builds up tension—it doesn't start out tense. When it comes to holding the club, there shouldn't be any "squeeze" to it at all. If you can feel even a modest amount of pressure in your forearms, you're squeezing the club too hard.

2. **You're tilting at windmills.** It's hard to say why exactly, but there are a whole bunch of golfers out there who suffer from something called a reverse pivot. It's an ugly sight, folks. In a proper swing, you start out with your weight fairly evenly distributed between your two legs. As the swing begins, your weight fairly quickly shifts into your right hip. In the downswing the weight shifts from the right hip into the left hip. The reverse pivot move is exactly the opposite. The golfer (not you, of course) somehow manages to get the weight into the left hip as the club starts back, causing the upper body to tilt toward

the target and making it impossible for any coiling action to occur. In the downswing the player must shift the other way (he'd fall over otherwise), and the result is a club being swung solely with the arms (no coil remember) and a golfer falling away from the target. Ouch. The poor guy has no chance of hitting a decent shot. To prevent this, key on shifting your weight into your right hip as the club starts back. Take caution not to let your weight shift turn into a body sway, where your hips move laterally outside your heels instead of over them. If you do that you'll lose coil and perhaps let your weight slip to the outside of your right leg, throwing you off balance.

3. **You're coming undone—and it ain't pretty.** If you've skipped around this book and missed the important stuff about how to build up power and then release it, go back. But before you do, know this: If you start your downswing with your arms or hands, you're dead. Done. Finished. Put a fork in yourself. Start the downswing from the ground up. Now go back and read the full explanation.

4. **You're playing footsies.** There are two things you can do with your feet that will sap your power supply: Point the tips of your toes directly at the target line, and let them lose contact with the ground. If the tips of your shoes point directly at the target line, you won't be able to do much more than slap the ball with your arms—that's if you don't fall over or drill yourself into the ground. Let the tips of your shoes flare out a bit—the right foot to the right just a shade, and the left foot to the left just a touch.

Keeping your feet rooted to the ground is another important element of creating power, but you see a lot of golfers who pull the left heel up in the backswing and the right heel up in the downswing. This can do some serious damage to the amount of tension you're capable of producing. To accommodate the shifting of your body's weight during your swing, think of "rolling" your weight to the insides of your feet, but keep those heels anchored to the ground.

5. **You're trying to kill it.** We know, we know. It sounds too simple. We can guarantee you that when you think "kill," the only thing you'll kill is your chances of hitting a good shot. Just think about this: How many times have you watched someone top the ball or hit a foot behind it and look up to say, "I was gonna kill that one." Your brain is a powerful weapon. Don't turn it against yourself. Rather, think of words like "turn" and "tempo." They'll do the trick.

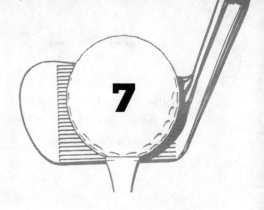

Practice

FORGET THE EXCUSES, WE'VE HEARD 'EM ALL. IF YOU DON'T PRACTICE, YOU WON'T IMPROVE. HERE'S HOW TO DO IT WITHOUT WASTING YOUR TIME.

There's an old story about Ben Hogan that is perhaps apocryphal but nevertheless makes a good point. The tale goes that a fellow professional golfer once approached Hogan and asked, "What's the secret, Mr. Hogan?" Hogan's response: "The answers are in the dirt." A man of few words, Hogan was simply trying to tell the young lad that the only way a player can improve his game is by practicing. Hogan's inference was specifically toward the idea of spending hour upon hour on the practice tee pounding balls from sun up until the twilight faded into night.

Nothing personal against Mr. Hogan, but other than going out on the course and actually playing, he didn't really have much else to do other than smash balls on the practice range all day. You don't hear many tales of Hogan (or any other tour golfer) having to take the kids to a Little League game, mowing the lawn, or taking the car in to have the brakes fixed. And while that's all well and good for them, we realize that unlike Hogan, Nicklaus, Woods, et al., you lead a life that simply doesn't allow for golf to be a single-minded pursuit. You have a limited amount of time to pursue your goal of breaking 100, so this chapter is going to help you use that time as wisely as possible.

Just What the Heck Am I Going to Accomplish by Practicing?

Everyone has a list of reasons for not practicing: It's boring. I don't have time. I don't know how. My dog ate it.

Well here's a revelation for you, partner. If you don't practice it's highly unlikely you're going to improve. We're guessing you don't have enough time to actually play a round every day of the week—you're probably lucky to get out once every two weeks or so. That's not enough frequency for you to see any improvement in your game. Only you have control over your time, but if you can steal the odd 30 minutes now and again *and* you have a definite goal in mind of what you are going to do with that 30 minutes, you will start to see some positive results. There's an old saying about practice that has been used to the point that it's a cliché, but it is true (as is the case with nearly every cliché). *Practice doesn't make perfect. Perfect practice makes perfect.* What this means is that hitting practice shots like you're at an artillery range is not only wasteful but could be damaging to your game. Those 30 minutes you managed to sneak aren't going to be of any use if you dump a bucket of balls on the ground and just start to lock, load, and fire, because when you're not engaged in a goal-directed activity, your mind wanders, making it easy for you to tinker yourself right out of a good golf swing. Or worse yet, ingrain bad habits and/or mechanics to the point that it will take a monumental effort to rid yourself of them.

We like to consider ourselves reasonable types, so we realize that the saying *"Perfect practice makes perfect"* is a bit daunting. After all, your goal is to break 100, not to win the Masters. (Not yet, anyway.) The idea of being "perfect" just isn't realistic, so we're going to modify it a bit so that it's applicable to you. Try this on for size: *Practice with a purpose leads to improvement.* Now that's a little easier to swallow, don't you think?

So what's your purpose—what's your goal? There are four basic goals you can use for any practice session. You can use them in any combination that seems good to you on a given day, depending upon how much time you have or what type of mood you're in. Just make sure to use at least one goal, because goals are the impetus behind human performance. And since you're human and you want to perform well, here are the four goals you can use while practicing:

1. Warming up:

Congratulations! You just met the requirements for practicing with a purpose, because every single practice session, even if it lasts only 10 minutes, should include some type of warm-up element. That's right: *Every single practice session should start with a warm-up.*

If you might think of your body as a machine for a moment (which, by the way, isn't a bad way to think of it all the time), it will make sense that you wouldn't just turn it on and say, "Okay body, do your thing. Golf that ball," primarily because an engine needs some time to get loose—to get the gas flowing through the lines, get that oil pumping, reach the optimal performance temperature, and do whatever else it is that engines do before they're ready for action. So even if you're just going to practice your short game for a little while, warm up first.

2. Putting the fun back into fundamentals:

All right, maybe that's a bit of a stretch, but every golfer has to work on the fundamentals. If you're a stone-cold beginner, you need to practice the fundamentals described in chapter 5 one by one. If you've been playing the game long enough to have a basic understanding of what you're supposed to be accomplishing with the fundamentals, you need to integrate them into a coherent whole, so when you think "fundamentals" you think of them as a single thing rather than individual items on a checklist. Even experts like Nick Faldo need to hone the fundamentals now and then to make sure that no imperfections have crept into their form.

3. Target orientation:

The third goal you can have for a practice session is getting zoned in on a target. In this type of practice, you work on hitting shots to a designated target, focusing only on the target. Prior to striking any ball in this type of practice, you should work through your entire pre-shot routine, including the very powerful element of visualization. This type of practice is the vital link that helps you take your game from the range to the course.

4. Practice as if you're playing:

You can actually play a round of golf right there on the practice range, using your imagination to lay out the course, going through your pre-shot routine and hitting the shots required given the situations you create in your mind. More than a few tour players do this prior to teeing it up in a competitive round. They know the course they're going to play, so they go through a dry run on the practice tee, hitting the shots in order, just as they would on the course. You can do this, too.

Now you know the four basic goals/types of practice you can focus on any time you practice. Let's take a closer look at each.

Warming Up

The purpose of the warm-up is to get the blood flowing into the muscles you need to execute the body mechanics necessary for golf. The purpose for the warm-up routine goes a bit deeper than that, however. It also puts you in the mood for what is about to occur, be it simply more practice or an actual round on the course. The warm-up allows you to put aside any non-golf-related concerns you may have lugged with you to the course, so your mind will be free to focus on the task at hand.

Your warm-up routine should be broken down into three substages, the length and importance of which you alone can judge. Nobody knows your strength and flexibility as well as you do, so you should personalize your warm-up routine to fit your needs. Here's the three stages you should concentrate on to get loose:

- **Stretching.** We could tell you how important this is until the cows come home and you still might think, "Ha, stretching is a waste of time." The next time you think that way, think about all the shots you fritter away on the first few holes because your body feels as stiff as Winston Churchill's upper lip. You need a quick program that works all the major muscle groups you need in golf. It'll help you play better and help you avoid ending up in traction. Read the sidebar on stretching. The reading is fast, and the routine itself probably won't even take you five minutes.

- **Swings without the ball.** Take a club and, starting slowly, make a continuous series of swings without stopping. Start at the address position and swing back as far as feels comfortable and through as far as feels comfortable. When you reach the end of the swing, just swing the club back again. And through again. Keep going for about a minute. Don't stop in the setup position; just keep that club moving.

- **Hit some balls, progressively.** You like to think of yourself as a progressive person, don't you? Here's a chance to put it in action. Take 10 balls out of your pile and start a series of progressively longer swings, culminating in full swings with the last two balls. You don't need your driver or any woods for this. In fact, stick to your wedges. On the first 3 balls, just try to flip them 20 yards or so. Try to hit the next 5 in increasing 10-yard increments. When you get to the last 2, hit full wedge shots.

    When you're hitting these 10 balls, it's important that you don't get too caught up in the idea of making pure contact with the ball. Nevertheless, we're well aware that there is something rather disheartening about hitting two inches behind the ball on your first few swings of the day, and there is something about the feel of a well-centered strike of the ball. (You didn't know we were brain specialists, did you?) So here's a tip: When you're hitting those 10 warm-up shots, put every one of them on a tee. This will help you avoid the distraction of possibly chunking the ball, and alleviate any worries about the lie, etc. Remember, you're just trying to get loose.

One final thought on warming up: It's a good idea to get to the course in time to hit a few balls before you play, *but take care not to turn your warm-up into a swing overhaul session. Don't search for a swing just before you go to the course. The best way to get ready to play is to do your stretching, and then to ready yourself for solid contact.*

HOW TO BECOME STRETCH ARM-STRONG IN FIVE MINUTES

People play golf for all sorts of reasons. Hopefully, your reason is to have fun. As such, we can assume you don't spend all of your waking hours preparing your body for battle. And unless you're a professional athlete, chances are pretty good that you don't realize the significant impact that stretching has on your game, especially early in a round. To be honest with you, we know it's important, but we thought you might pay a little more attention to this if we asked an expert to give you a quick routine. So we asked our buddy Jennifer Haigh, the fitness editor of *Men's Health* magazine, to whip up an easy-to-understand, easy-to-do stretching routine for you. She's a lot smarter than us and she spends a lot of time thinking about stuff like this, so pay attention. If you don't, she promises to be at the first tee to laugh at you when you flub your opening tee shot. Here's her advice, all of which simulates movements in an actual golf swing. (See, we told you she was smart.)

- **Do some necking.** That got your attention, heh? Okay, what you want to do here is turn your head to the right, looking as far over your shoulder as possible. (While you're at it, you can check to make sure Lenny isn't stealing any balls out of your bag.) Now take your left hand and push gently against the left side of your face. Hold this for 10–15 seconds, then switch sides.

- **Go shoulder to shoulder with yourself.** Reach across your body with your left arm and grab the back of your right elbow with your left hand. Now stretch your right arm across your body, getting it under your chin if you can. Hold it for 10 seconds. Then do it to the other arm.

- **Stick that chest out.** Clasp your hands behind your back, and raise your arms up and out. Inhale to increase the stretch.

- **Take care of the bends.** Hmm. It's not as bad as it sounds. Bend forward, ever so gently, from your waist and grasp your ankles. If you need to flex your knees to do so, have at it. Let your neck and arms relax as you bend forward slowly from your hips. Still hanging onto those ankles? Good. Now straighten your knees until you feel a comfortable stretch in the backs of your legs. Hold this for 10–15 seconds, then let go of your ankles and *slowly* raise yourself up, bending your knees as you straighten your trunk.

- **Is that a body in your trunk?** This will help loosen the trunk of your body. Standing with your back to a tree or a golf cart, rotate your upper body to the right, so you can grab hold of the tree or cart with both hands without moving your feet. Look over your left shoulder as you do this. You can increase the tension by pulling yourself around a little farther with your hands. Hold for 10–15 seconds, then repeat with the other side.

- **All golfers love a little side action.** Stand with your feet shoulder-width apart and raise your right arm above your head. Keeping your knees slightly flexed, lean to your left and slide your left hand down the outside of your left thigh to just above your knee. You should feel a comfortable stretch along the left side of your torso. Hold it for 10–15 seconds, then repeat on the other side.

Working on Those Oh So *Fundamentals*

Our work with countless students just like you has shown us that up to 80 percent of all errors in the full swing are the result of a lack of attention to the details in the setup fundamentals. Since your aspiration is to break 100, you should concentrate on nailing down the fundamentals. The foundations of a solid swing—the *fundamental* building blocks—are your grip, stance, posture, ball position, and aiming and alignment. These are all covered in earlier sections of this book.

When you decide to work on your fundamentals, make no mistake about it, *the practice tee is the only place for it.* Either on your own or under the guidance of a competent teacher/coach of the game, the practice tee is the place where you isolate the elements of your fundamentals for specific attention. Here's something to keep in mind: When you're doing this sort of "piecework" evaluation of your fundamentals, it's not the ball flight by which you should judge the effectiveness. Judge the effectiveness by how cognizant you are of each fundamental and how persistent you are at remembering to check each element.

When you're working on your fundamentals it's an excellent idea to set up a little "workout" station. To do this take three clubs and lay them on the ground as follows: One club just on the outside of your target line (so that the ball will sit on the ground on the inside of the club in relation to your body); one club parallel to the first club, lying just along the tips of your toes; the third club lying perpendicular to the first club along the point where you want to position the ball in your stance, on the side opposite the ball. Use the first club to check your acclimation to the target line and the aim of your clubface; use the second club to check the alignment of your feet, parallel to the target line; use the third club to ensure consistent positioning of the ball. You should also hit every shot off a tee. By doing this, your mind is free to focus on what your body is doing and not worrying about getting the ball airborne.

Fundamentals also include things such as working on the idea of turning away from the ball and leading the downswing with your hips. Once again, don't worry about ball flight. Focus

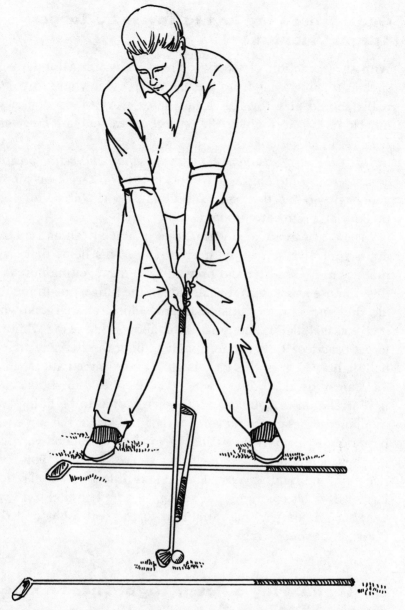

The basic practice station: club to indicate target line; club to square feet to; club perpendicular for ball position, midway between feet and ball.

and concentrate on the "feel" of the action you're working on— on what your body is doing.

Getting Used to Playing Toward a Target: Target Orientation

With the exception of when you're working on a fundamental such as turning away from the ball or grooving your tempo, you really should play towards a target for every practice shot you hit. Here's a rule for you: *In general, when you're taking target practice, don't be concerned with your swing, and when you're working on swing fundamentals other than the setup position, don't focus on the target.* If while working on target orientation you begin to hit the ball exceedingly poorly, abandon target practice and return to fundamental practice.

The best way to keep your target practice fresh and interesting is to switch targets with every shot. This helps make your practice more realistic and prevents you from getting bored. Try this: Choose a target on the left side of the range, one in the middle, and one on the right side. Change clubs (and targets) whenever you feel like it, and don't think about your swing while you target practice. Rather than thinking about the swing, watch the ball flight, which in this case is giving you immediate feedback. You can adjust accordingly when you see how your shots are flying in relation to your target. If you're going to be doing some fundamental practice and some target practice at the same time, be certain to keep them distinct in your mind. A good way to do this is to announce to yourself that you're switching your practice type, and remind yourself what sort of feedback you're looking for (if you're working on "swing," ignore ball flight; if you're working on "target," pay attention to the ball flight and don't think about your swing).

Go Ahead, Play a Round Right There on the Practice Tee

They say the longest walk in golf is the one from the practice tee to the first tee. It is during this walk that a metamorphosis takes place, which can be described as nothing less than, well, stupid. If you've played for any length of time, you've almost certainly experienced the All-World Range Player Phenomenon. It works like this: You hit it great on the practice tee and are brimming with confidence. You get to the first tee and proceed to play like you're wearing a straight jacket. What happened? Something along these lines, friend: Once you get out on the course, there's a one-ball success rate—you get one try on each shot, and Mr. Brain knows it. But when you stand on the practice tee clobbering ball after ball with the same club, you're giving yourself multiple chances for success. Our suggestion is to devote a fair amount of your practice time to gearing up your brain for the one-ball success rate you need to play the game—in other words, practice like you play. Here's how:

Place your bag, with all of your clubs in it, next to your practice station. Then begin to visualize a course with which you're very familiar. Each "hole" you play should have a specific yardage, so even if you can't recall the actual yardage of a hole you played, assign it one for the purposes of this practice. Here's a sample hole: Let's say it's a 400-yard par four with a slight dogleg to the right. You choose the club you're comfortable with from the tee (don't automatically reach for the driver) and pick a spot on the left side of the "fairway" as your target. (Think about making a purposeful practice swing at this point, visualizing the shot and preparing your mind to play it.) Now you go through your pre-shot routine and get yourself set to play toward that target. Then you play the shot. Now let's say you made solid contact, but you pulled it a little, so the ball landed in the left "rough" as opposed to the "fairway." Now you'd make your best estimation on the club you'll need for the second shot. Remember to take into account the fact that you're in the rough, any big wind factors, any hazards you might have to carry, etc. On this particular hole, it turns out there is a creek crossing the fairway about 20 yards shy of the green. Given the lie and the fact that, perhaps, there's a slight breeze in your face, you decide you're going to lay up short of the creek, playing a shot of approximately 150 yards. You take the club you think will fly the ball 150 yards, and you now have about 50 yards left to the green. Then you select a target, set up, and play a 50-yard pitch shot. And so on. If you have the time, play an entire "round" on your favorite "course." (Heck, if you've watched the Masters enough on TV, you could play Augusta National's back nine without shelling out those expensive membership fees.) This type of practice is a fun way to squeeze in a "quick 18." (To add to the fun, give yourself an automatic two-putt on each green to see what you might have shot.)

And Now a Word from Your Short Game: Don't Forget, More Than 60 Percent of Your Shots Are from 100 Yards or Closer

As noted earlier in this book, more than 60 percent of the shots you play in a round of golf are from within 100 yards of the hole, including chips, pitches, bunker shots, and putts. It only makes sense that a certain amount of your time should be spent practicing these things. Does it need to be 60 percent? At the outset of your quest to break 100, absolutely. You should consider short game practice part of your fundamental practice, and it's quite a good way to work on your alignment skills. It's easier to get comfortable aimed at a target that's only 30 yards away or so. *At the very least you should devote at least half your time to practicing your short game (don't forget the bunker shots!), especially early in the developmental stages of your game.* Frankly speaking, once you get your short game rolling, it requires less maintenance than the long game. As a result, as your game improves you can spend less and less time on it, *but you should never completely stop practicing it.* In fact, if everything works out great and you become a tour player a few years after reading this book, you'll find yourself going the other way—practicing the short game more and more.

Going Mental

We don't want to get weird on you or anything, but a big part of determining whether you succeed or fail in golf is dependent upon what's going on between your ears. The good news in golf is that you don't have to avoid 250-pound linebackers who can run a 2.3 in the 40, return rocket serves from Pete Sampras, or recoil in fear as Charles Barkley thunders a slam that lands on your head. The bad news is, you have something much more powerful to contend with—your brain. We can't do much in a book to help your on-course demeanor other than to encourage you not to get discouraged by bad shots. One good one can make up for a couple of bad ones. What we can do to help your quest to break 100, however, is to encourage you to use that powerful brain of yours to your advantage when you're nowhere near a golf course or a practice range.

One of the best ways to work on your game is away from the golf course using a combination of full-body relaxation plus mental imagery, a technique similar to those the Eastern Europeans have used for years in some of their Olympic training programs. You can easily learn to summon a deep state of relaxation and then imagine practicing or playing a round of golf, shot by shot. And we promise it won't turn you into a champion Greco-Roman wrestler. This type of mental practice is a great way to stay sharp, especially if you live somewhere with inclement weather during the winter months.

The first step in the technique (the relaxation part) was popularized by Harvard heart specialist Herbert Benson. In his best-selling book, *The Relaxation Response,* Benson described the ability of patients to lower their blood pressure by using some simple relaxation procedures. With a few minor modifications the same thing can be adapted to improve your golf game. Here's how:

- Find a quiet place where you won't be disturbed. Assume a sitting position with your legs folded and crossed in front of you and your spine straight, resting against a wall or a tree. It helps if you use earplugs, because it's easier to isolate the sound of your breathing, a key element of the procedure.

- Inhale through your nostrils so that your breath fills your stomach. Once your abdominal cavity is filled, continue your breath and fill your upper chest cavity.

- Once you've filled your body with air (remember, first abdominal, then your chest), force the air out through your mouth using your stomach muscles. Place your hand on your abdomen to feel it swell as you breathe in and contract as you breathe out. Once you get the rhythm, relax and focus on the sound of your breathing to the exclusion of everything else.

- Continue as in step two until you're in a complete state of relaxation. At first, it might take you 15 minutes or more to get completely relaxed, but as you become more adept, you can do it in less than a minute.

- Now it's time to play a little golf. Let's say you need some practice hitting your driver. Imagine yourself addressing the ball. Feel, see, and hear everything about the scene. The solidness of your stance, the gracefulness of your backswing, the controlled power of your downswing, the squareness of contact, the flight of the ball, and of course, where your ball comes to rest. The more precise you make your image, the more effective your mental practice becomes. And after you practice, you can play a few holes or even an entire round of golf using your power of mental imagery. Many of golf's greatest players—from Hogan to Nicklaus—have used mental techniques to maximize their performance. With a little practice, you, too, can add the advantages of "mental" practice to your game.

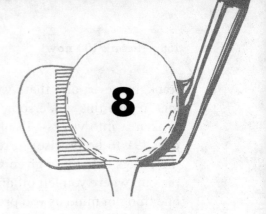

8

It's Time to Stop Reading and Start Doing

At the very beginning of this book we told you we'd give you a calendar to follow, so it would be easier to stay on track on your quest to break 100. That's what we're going to do right here. It's not a day-to-day calendar, because that would just be silly. You don't know what days you're going to have time to do things, so to ask you to do things on a daily basis would simply be nonsense. We also realize that you're not going to stop playing actual rounds of golf and concentrate solely on practicing for three months. The intent, then, of this calendar, is for you to use it as a progressive guide or a reminder of things you should be working on at any given time. We can't help you find the time to do it, so you're on your own there. We can help keep you on track, however, and that's what you should get out of this chapter. To give this guide some sense of chronological order, we've broken it into weeks—13 of them—which gives you roughly 90 days (91 to be precise) to reach your goal. If you can get to all the things listed in a given week, that's terrific. If you can't, just pick up where you left off and keep on trucking. And please keep one thing in mind as you practice: It's best to approach each task separately rather than attempting to do a whole bunch together. It gets too confusing if you try to do many things at once. So pick a task, work on it, finish it, then move on to the next one.

Week One

Now is the time to review your arsenal. So go back to chapter 2 and review the elements of your set makeup that you should check in detail.

- Check the loft on your driver. If the degree of loft isn't stamped on it somewhere, have a pro measure it for you. Remember, too little loft is a big mistake. If you don't like what you have, hold an "audition." Try out all kinds of demo models. Ask for some impact tape and check how often you hit each one in the center of the clubface.

- Consider dumping the long irons from your set and replacing them with high-lofted fairway woods. (It's up to you, of course, but we say if you don't have a 7-wood, you're doing yourself a serious injustice.)

- Check your wedges. If you don't have a sand wedge, get one. Think about adding an L-wedge (60 degrees or more) to your set.

- Have a clubfitter or golf professional check the shafts in your clubs for two things: Are they the proper flex for you? Do they match throughout your set? (Not just the irons, but the woods, too?) Another way of doing this is to hit various demo clubs and hit the clubs of some of your friends. Try all of the basic flexes: regular, stiff, extra stiff, seniors. If you're a woman, ask about women's flexes. And while you're at the clubfitter, have the lie of your irons checked as well.

- Are your grips the proper size? If you think they're too small, wrap some gauze around them and hit some practice shots. Feel good? Maybe you need bigger grips.

Week Two

- Finish up anything having to do with your set makeup. If you're not comfortable with what you have or what you've tried, keep searching. And speaking of grips (well, we were two sentences ago), if you haven't had yours changed in the past year, they're worn out. Get new ones.

- Choose your ball. You're going to play a two-piece surlyn type, but which one? Buy three major brands and take them to the practice area. Play some pitch shots, hit some chips, and roll a whole bunch of putts, all the time monitoring them for feel and control. They'll all perform nearly the same on long shots, but from close in you may detect some difference in the feel. Use the one that feels best.

- Kick-start your brain. Start to think about the relative strengths and weaknesses of your game in preparation for creating your strength and weakness profile.

- Find a place where you can practice regularly. At the very least it should have a place to hit full shots and a practice green. A practice bunker is also nice. Get to know the people at the course/facility. They'll be much more accommodating once they know you.

Week Three

- If you've finished up with the details regarding your clubs, that's great. If not, get it done. Playing with clubs that don't fit you or your swing is like trying to hit a Roger Clemens fastball with a wiffle ball bat.

- Are you a right-arm dominant putter, or a left-arm dominant putter? Figure it out, and then make sure you're using the proper type of putter for your stroke.

- Start to get the distance of your putts under control. Remember: Distance is more important than direction in putting. Use the techniques described early in chapter 3 to start getting the ball closer to the hole.

- Start to organize the rest of your short game in your mind. Do you know the difference between a chip and a pitch? Do you know the situations that call for you to putt? To chip? To pitch?

- Whether playing or practicing, remember this mantra: Putt whenever you can, chip only when you can't putt, and pitch only when you can't chip.

Week Four

- Start spending some time around the sides of the practice green, concentrating on getting the correct distance on your chips with the 5-iron, 7-iron, and 9-iron. Are you making sure to get the club up on its toe *every time?* Make checking this a part of your routine.

- Are you familiar and comfortable with the technique for playing consistently good chip shots? If not, it's time to start concentrating on it.

- Start to practice getting the ball in the hole on the practice green. Drop 10 balls around the hole in a three-foot circle. Practice going around and around until you can hole out all 10 putts in succession. If you miss, start again.

- Some pitches sit, some walk, and some run. When you're playing, start to identify situations and mentally picture which type of pitch shot would be appropriate.

- Try to squeeze in a practice session that concentrates solely on becoming familiar with exactly how far you hit each club under optimum conditions.

- While you're at the range, start practicing the three types of pitch shots. You don't need to hit them to a green or to see the results at this point. Just start practicing the setup and the motion.

- After you've completed any full round, begin a routine of tallying up the total number of putts you used during the round. Your eventual goal should be to get that total down to 36 putts per round.

Week Five

- Continue working on becoming familiar with the distance you hit each club.

- Begin concentrating on your sand game. If you still don't have a sand wedge, get one. Otherwise, forget about breaking 100.

- Remember: From the sand, your first basic goal is to get out of the sand and onto the green in one shot. Anywhere on the green. So work on developing a shot you can hit 20–30 feet from the sand. Out on the course, use this shot any time you get in the sand near the green. Ignore the hole and play to the center of the green.

- Off the course, familiarize yourself with and practice the idea of Face + Base + Pace. Use this to work toward playing your sand shots toward the hole.

- Start the mental process of acknowledging that, for the time being and until you can consistently break 100, your concept of par (Personal Par) and the par indicated on the scorecard are not the same thing.

- How's that putting coming along? To get comfortable with the idea of using 36 putts, do a circuit of 18 holes on the practice green using only one ball. Keep after it until you can do this circuit fairly regularly in 36 strokes or less.

- Out on the course start to take note of this: On driving holes (par fours and par fives), how many times does your drive land in the fairway? Keep track over a couple of rounds. And out of the times you miss the fairway, keep track of how many times you hit your driver.

- Start using the three different types of pitches on the course.

Week Six

- Become familiar with the idea of Personal Par and start using it on the course. If you can't remember the determining factors, write them down on an index card and fold it up with the scorecard in your pocket or clip it to the scorecard holder on your cart.

- By now you should have completed the practice that determined how far you hit each club. If you haven't, make sure you get it done before moving into your new way of "managing" your game on the course. You can't do the second (manage your game) without the first (knowing how far you hit the ball).

- How many fairways are you hitting? If you're hitting them all, that's stupendous. If your tee shots are continually getting you into trouble, it's time you start considering your options from the tee. There's no rule that says you must hit driver on every long hole. Try your 3-wood, or your 5-wood, or even your 7-wood if you want to—just get the ball in the fairway.

- Start thinking like a pro. Learn to determine and play for the true yardage, not the measured yardage. Review the tips in chapter 4 if you forgot them.

- Start assessing holes from "dot to dot" rather than being led along by the design of the hole. Remember, the course architect intends for his designs to challenge your mind, and the first assumption they make is that you won't think beyond grabbing for your driver. Outsmart them.

- How's that sand game coming? If you can't find a practice bunker, find a friendly local pro who will let you practice out on the course either early in the day or late in the afternoon. Early in the day the last hole on each nine are empty for nearly two hours. Late in the day, the first hole on each nine is empty for a few hours, too. Smile, be nice, act pathetic, do whatever it takes. Get some time in the sand.

- Still not down to 36 putts yet? Could be because you haven't gotten your lag putting under control yet. Try this: Go to the practice green and take nine balls with you. Stick a tee in the ground 10 feet from your pile. Stick another tee in the ground 20 feet from your pile, and another tee 35 feet from your pile. Now putt the first three balls to the closest tee, the next three to the intermediate tee, and the last three to the farthest tee. Keep repeating this until you can cluster all three groups near their target. Once you've done that, break it up as follows: Hit one ball to the near tee, the next to the intermediate tee, and the next to the farthest tee. Then go back to the near tee. This is more realistic for what you might face on the course.

Week Seven

- Put together your strength and weakness profile. *Be honest with yourself.* Check chapter 4 if you forget how. If you've been keeping track of the number of fairways you hit from the tee, that's definitely a part of your strength and weakness profile.

- Determine your "go to" clubs.

- You should be feeling comfortable with the concept of Personal Par by now. If you're not, get over it. Remember: Actual par is a system for comparing the performance of expert players. Are you an expert golfer? Do you compare your performance in other recreational pursuits to that of experts?

- Continue the evolution of your ability to properly assess on-course situations. Start to put to use the "red light, yellow light, green light" system of assessing situations. Combine this with the idea of playing "dot to dot."

- Design a simple Personal Par scorecard or sheet that you can copy on a copying machine. It should have a box for the hole, the length, the Personal Par you assigned it, your actual score, fairways hit from the tee, the number of putts on each hole, whether you hit the green in regulation for your Personal Par, successful escapes from bunker (in one shot), and one box that simply indicates whether you hit each shot good or not. You can use this to identify areas of your game that need attention. Use this sheet on the course rather than the actual scorecard. (You can fill in the details while you're waiting around.) Do it for every round you play.

- Don't ignore your short game. Can you make those pitches sit, walk, and run? Try practicing with a friend. Let them call out a shot and then you try to hit it. Another variation is you set up to hit one of the three and see if they can guess which one you're going to play.

Week Eight

- Time to start checking the fundamentals of your long game. Start with your grip. If your grip isn't proper and comfortable, you've got a major problem.

- Become cognizant of *where* and *how* you're aiming for every single shot you play on the course. Begin to develop a pre-shot routine.

- You're becoming a better manager every day. Start to manage your game before you go to the course. Going to play a course you know is tight? Take the driver out of the bag before you leave the house. Toss in an extra wedge (if you have one).

- Down to 36 putts a round yet? Try this drill: Start with three balls about one foot from the hole. Make all three putts. Move back to 2 feet. Make all three. If you miss one, it's back to the one-footer. If you make all three 2-footers, move on to the 3-foot range. Any time you miss, start over. Keep going until you get to 10 feet, then work your way back toward the hole.

Week Nine

- In every round you now play you should be employing all of the tactics you know for managing your game. Concentrate on Personal Par—don't use it as an imaginary goal that you should simply be satisfied with. Use it as an actual goal you're excited about. Play every round from now until the end of the cycle using the "red light, yellow light, green light" system. You should be mentally breaking holes down into manageable shot combinations now, i.e., two accurate 7-wood shots are safer and more consistent than a driver and a 6-iron are likely to be.

- Play an entire round by deciding which club to hit and then actually hitting one more club. See what happens. Are you correctly judging the actual distance? If you are closer to the hole/green more often during this round, you may need to start being more realistic with your club selection.

- Start to devote some practice time to working on fundamentals: Grip, stance, aiming. Start to work on the concept of "coil" on the practice tee. Don't pay attention to ball flight.

Week Ten

- You should have a solid pre-shot routine by now, and you should start to use it before every single shot you play on the course *and* on the practice tee.

- Hopefully you're not still floundering in the sand. If you are, try this: When you stick the club too deep into the sand it makes a *thud*, and when you hit one good it sounds like *pffffffffff*. Go into a practice bunker once in a while without a ball. Purposely hit too much sand and become familiar with the sound of a heavy shot. Then make swings that take the proper amount of sand and become familiar with that sound. When you prepare to play an actual shot during a round, "hear" the sound of a good shot before you play it.

- Update your strength and weakness profile. Draw some conclusions. Work on areas that need help.

- On the practice tee, start to work on the concept of a smooth transition from downswing to backswing. Don't worry about ball flight.

- Get comfortable with your personal tempo and put it to use in your game.

Week Eleven

- Start to use the stats you've been compiling on your Personal Par scoresheet. Draw some conclusions and put them to use in your game. Example: "I'm not a good long iron player, because according to my stats I hit a good long iron only once out of every six tries. I can't rely on them. The shot I'm about to play is long iron distance and there's water off to the right. I'm going to be smart and lay up." Now you're thinking.

- Start to practice like you're playing an actual round. See chapter 7 if you forgot the concept.

- Before you play, get loose. Make the stretching routine from chapter 7 part of every pre-practice and pre-round routine.

- Take the ideas of "coil" and "tempo" to the course with you. However, don't think about them specifically on the course. Instead, just think about swinging through to a nice, balanced finish. You're not in any hurry to hit the ball.

Week Twelve

- Be certain to delineate between "target" practice and "swing" practice. During "target" practice, you don't think about your swing; during "swing" practice, the target should be out of mind.

- Being careful to segment the practice sessions as indicated above, continue working on the weak areas as indicated by your Personal Par scoresheet.

- On the course, don't play "golf swing." Just concentrate on the numbers and play "target." Map your route to the hole target by target and hit them. "Target" golf is like "target" practice—you don't think about mechanics. If you start thinking mechanics out on the course, you're dead. If someone starts chattering to you about your swing, walk away or politely tell them to shut up.

- Continually update your strength and weakness profile vis-à-vis monitoring your stats. Continue to concentrate on the weak areas.

Week Thirteen

- You're a thinking machine. You're a world-class manager. You know your strengths and you play to them. You set your own standards, you don't play to someone else's. You keep your cool when things go wrong—one bad shot doesn't ruin the hole. You're ready. Go and do it. And have fun.

Afterthought

Hopefully, this book will help you achieve your goal of breaking 100. Even if you don't manage to do it in 90 days, the stuff in this book will help get you there eventually. It really comes down to how much time you put into it. Like anything else, in golf you reap what you sow. In golf, however, the reaping requires a little more time and a lot more patience than just about any other game. After all, you're competing with yourself. When you do finally reach your goal, we can promise you one thing—the quest will have been worth it. Good luck.